Praise for Arlene's first book,
Moving Forward: The Widow's Journey

"A deeply moving and helpful book."

— Verified Amazon buyer

"The universal appeal of this book can't be overstated, and its message can't be understated."

— Verified Amazon buyer

"It is simultaneously practical and inspirational, providing the reader with strategies for living a life of strength and purpose while handling the challenges that come with the reality of living alone."

— Verified Amazon buyer

"Arlene's book is so well-written and the concept of using different widows' stories means there's different perspectives and experiences to learn from. If you experience bereavement from the loss of someone very close, the message of moving forward rather than moving on is so understandable and relatable."

— Attendee at Books & Books

"The death of a loved one is something we will all have to face sometime in our lifetime. It was a lovely day of learning and sharing with friends. All attending expressed that they were glad they had read the book and that they learned from it."

— Los Angeles Book Club member

"*Moving Forward* by Arlene Sacks was an unbelievable help and amazing for anyone grieving a loved one, particularly anyone who has lost a life partner or anyone supporting someone who is recently widowed."

— Reddit member

"Arlene Sacks has beautifully written about her journey along with vignettes on other women. I have recommended this book to a few of my widow clients who are starting a support group. As a counselor, I highly recommend this book as a tool to help others walk this trail with support, knowing they are not alone."

— Goodreads

THE
ALCHEMY
OF **LOVE** &
MARRIAGE

How We Repaired the Cracks and Cemented Our Bond

Author of *Moving Forward*

DR. ARLENE SACKS

REDWOOD PUBLISHING, LLC

Published by Redwood Publishing, LLC
Orange County, California
www.redwooddigitalpublishing.com

ISBN: 978-1-956470-97-0 (hardcover)
ISBN: 978-1-956470-96-3 (paperback)
ISBN: 979-8-9906149-5-6 (e-book)
ISBN: 978-1-956470-98-7 (audiobook)

Library of Congress Control Number: 2024919353

Cover Design by Michelle Manley of Graphique Designs
Interior Book Design by Jose Pepito
Illustrations by Rein G. (reindrawthings)
Editing by Avery Auer

To my muse,

A muse sparks something inside that gives you the desire and the passion to create. I dedicate this book to my muse who helped me move from developing a concept to creating this book. You never ceased to provide the confidence I needed to complete my work.

ONCE UPON A TIME

The phrase *Once upon a time* usually introduces a fairy tale. This book is not a fairy tale, but it is a tale—and by that, I mean a story. It tells of two people who met, were enchanted by that chemistry of youth, and after four years of dating, married. Together, they grew as a couple, moving from initial passion to friendship and trust. They had children and lived a life that seemed to de-

velop in a rather traditional way. Their children became adults, found partners, got married, and created their own families.

Then one day, the two people were just two again. They were still passionate about each other and their work, had time to travel, en-

joyed peace and quiet, and even had some disposable income. They were fine; life was good. And then it was not. It was not illness that threatened their relationship or any one thing they could pinpoint. It was that dark outside storm that hits like a tornado: life itself.

CONTENTS

Part 3

The Next Twenty Years

PREFACE

THE MAGIC OF THE PROPOSAL AND THE LOGIC OF LIFE

"Challenges are what makes life interesting, and overcoming them is what makes life meaningful."

—Joshua J. Marine, author

The night Howard and I got engaged unfolded like a scaled-down version of what would eventually be our marriage experience as a whole. It modeled the sequence of events in our larger story. The beginning of that evening was full of light, almost like a fairy tale. The middle was when darkness entered. And at the end, we made the choice to go back into the light. I would like to share the details with you.

When Howard decided to propose to me, just about four years into our relationship, he planned the entire evening perfectly. He arrived at the apartment I shared with my parents, bouquet of flowers and wrist corsage in hand, and off we went for a special evening in New York City. It was not a bad beginning for a twenty-year-old college senior and his nineteen-year-old girlfriend.

Our first stop was the Tower Suite, a most elegant restaurant atop the Time & Life Building and a far cry from our usual diners and cafeterias. Howard had reserved a table next to the huge windows overlooking Radio City Music Hall and Fifth Avenue. As we scrutinized the fancy menu, three waiters stood by to serve us.

Two hours later, sated and content, we strolled through Central Park. In the middle of a bridge over the lake, Howard told me to stop for a second. He then got down on one knee, pulled a tiny box from his breast pocket, and proposed—and I said yes.

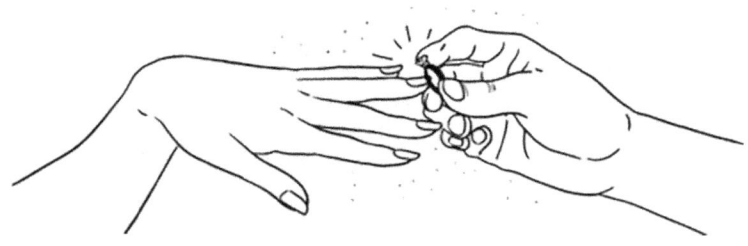

After sealing the deal with a passionate embrace, we continued our walk hand in hand, exiting the park in front of the legendary Plaza Hotel. Just like in the movies, Howard gestured toward a beautiful horse-drawn carriage. I stepped up into it and settled back into the plush seat, admiring the ring now twinkling on my finger.

Sounds like a fairy tale evening, right? So far, so good.

Once we were both settled, the driver offered us a coarse wool blanket to lay across our legs, and we arranged it. Within a minute, just as we were noticing a foul odor emanating from the thing, we were both scratching madly at our skin.

Unaware of the drama unfolding in the back, the driver shouted something to the horse, flipped the reins, and off we went. And I mean *off!* Our promised forty-five-minute jaunt around the park would take approximately eight. Clearly inebriated, our driver shouted and prodded at the horse until we were flying past pedestrians, bicyclists, and other carriages. Silently, Howard and I gripped each other's hands and prayed that the first night of the rest of our lives would not be the last.

The moment we arrived back in front of the Plaza, the two of us bolted from the carriage and ran to the corner still holding onto each other, breathless and laughing all the way. The ride had not gone as planned, but it was over, and the fun, laughter, and great story remained.

As we made our way down Fifth Avenue, we slowed our pace, and I could not help grinning and waving my newly decorated ring finger at passersby. The few people left on the street paid absolutely no attention, but I did not care a bit. I was a young girl out with my fiancé. The city was ours, and we were ready to take life on and chart our course together.

Just as we would in our marriage, we had started off strong, weathered a daunting experience, and come out the other side smiling. We had decided not to dwell on the darkness but to follow the light.

Much later, when I thought back on that eventful night, I recalled something Joan Didion wrote in her essay "Goodbye to All That": "One of the mixed blessings of being twenty and twenty-one and even twenty-three is the conviction that nothing like this, all evidence to the contrary notwithstanding, has ever happened to anyone before."

The bricks come apart. Can they be recemented?

> "Out of suffering have emerged the strongest souls; the most massive characters are seared with scars."
>
> —Kahlil Gibran, Lebanese American writer and poet

In this book, I will share with you one of the most challenging experiences life can present: the potential implosion of a marriage and the process of coming together to save it. I call it a *story*, but it is my *true* story, and therefore mine to share. My husband, Howard, and I may sometimes appear to be its heroes, but I assure you, we were not. We were just two people trying to get through life.

It is my honor to travel the road of my marriage experience with you—from where it began to where it ended—and it is my mission to share the wisdom I attained along that road. In that way, I suppose you could call this book a "teachable memoir." I offer it to you not as a psychologist, religious leader, philosopher, or doctor but as a caring, thinking person just like you, who was fortunate enough to enjoy a forty-seven-year marriage before my widowhood in 2013. Over the long arc of that relationship, my husband and I grew, changed, learned things, made mistakes, laughed, cried, and ultimately created something greater than ourselves.

Howard and I experienced ecstatic highs and abysmal lows, and I believe it is essential to present both ends of that spectrum honestly—not just the positive side. After all, if I held back the "bad" and the "ugly," my story would not be entirely honest—and then what would be the point in sharing it? It is in those moments when life is on the line and we genuinely have something to lose that we remember the preciousness of what we have. That is when we figure out how to fight for the life we love.

Having emphasized that my story is true, I agree with a comment I once heard Nigerian American writer Hafizah Augustus Geter make during a TV interview: "There are always multiple truths." This book tells *my* truth about things that happened to Howard and me in our early, middle, and later years. I think of the events as bricks in our road together, at the end of which we had attained true friendship, trust, and the deepest love possible. It is my hope that in reading it, you will find things that relate to your own journey and perhaps some lessons you can apply to your own life.

No one book or personal story can fully express the experience of marriage. But, having enjoyed a long, eventful, complex, and ultimately satisfying marriage, I like to think that my story is worth telling—and worth hearing.

—Arlene Sacks, January 2024

PART 1

THREE WAYS TO LOOK AT MARRIAGE

*"And when you want something, all the universe
conspires in helping you achieve it."*

—Paulo Coelho, *The Alchemist*

While a secret is meant to remain just that, sometimes it is important to share one. Now that you, the reader, are part of my world, you are going to learn some of my secrets about marriage in general, and mine in particular.

For me, marriage is an ongoing balance between magic and logic. All of life is a balancing act, from what we eat to how we manage our relationships. Some of us are good at balancing; some, less so. But love maintained over a long marriage (or even a short one) involves that magic-logic balance. It is forever.

CHAPTER 1

WHAT IS ALCHEMY?

"You are an alchemist; make gold of that."
—William Shakespeare, *Timon of Athens,* act 5, scene 1

I have used the word *alchemy* in my title, and you will come across it throughout the book, but what does this term that I am using metaphorically actually refer to?

Quite simply, alchemy was the predecessor of chemistry. It involves combining various materials or elements that might be weak or strong on their own into something greater. It has come to be thought of as the process of turning base metals into gold.

Because gold was highly valued in the ancient world, alchemists were revered by kings, queens, and rulers throughout the world. They were given laboratories in which to experiment and encouraged to produce gold by whatever means necessary. Through the centuries, our love of precious metals has not abated; we compete for gold medals, offer our loved ones gold rings, and fill our stories with geese that lay golden eggs and wars fought over a golden fleece.

The alchemy of marriage can be looked at as a similar process with equally valuable results. If we can combine the many elements of our lives in just the right way, we can create the "gold standard" of relationships: a rich, strong, and satisfying marriage that lasts a lifetime. In other words, we can transform the base materials of ourselves and our lives into something invaluable.

This process may be somewhat mysterious, but it is not magic. Rather, it is based on choices. Exactly which elements will produce the desired outcome—the "gold"? With thought, commitment, and care, the right decisions can be made, leading to a successful process. But whether the outcome is a golden success or a failure, at least the attempt was made. As author Sean Covey puts it in his book *The 7 Habits of Highly Effective Teens*, "We are free to choose our paths, but we can't choose the consequences that come with them."

My own marriage story is just one example of the human alchemical process, but I think it is an instructive one. When it became necessary, Howard and I embarked on the great experiment. We made difficult, soul-searching choices. We opened ourselves to personal change. And, in the end, we produced something more precious than either of us could have foreseen. I have discovered that the only predictable parts of our marriage were the changes we both experienced as time marched on.

CHAPTER 2

THE GREEKS' SIX
STAGES OF LOVE

*"The ancient Greeks knew love could be
discovered not just with a sexual partner, but
also in friendships, amongst strangers, and with
themselves. Love is cultivated in many forms."*

—Roman Krznaric, "Finding the True Meaning of Love"

The ancient Greeks—from whom we have much to learn—came up with what they called the six stages of love, and I have found these very helpful in codifying contemporary marriage. As I studied each of them, I began to understand that they are actually a hierarchy and that one leads to the next (with some overlap as they proceed). This lit up a light bulb in my head; it made so much sense! I realized that as my marriage to Howard had progressed, we had gone through each of the Greeks' stages, from the very beginning of intimacy all the way to the end.

So, why had we encountered problems? In analyzing my marriage through this lens, it became clear to me that when Howard and I had experienced difficulty progressing from one stage to the next, there had been negative consequences. While we had proceeded through some of the stages quite organically, we had faltered in others. Unless we could figure out where we had gotten bogged down, our life together was in peril.

I am aware that the Greeks' six stages of love are also referred to as "types" of love; however, I choose to use the term "stages" deliberately in order to parallel them to the stages in our marriage—the early, middle, and later years—thereby dividing the six stages (two within each of the stages of our marriage). We will look at the six stages one by one:

1. **Eros,** the first stage, is the most basic. It is defined as sensual or passionate love—thus *erotic*. It is associated with romance and fairy tales, where the attraction is intense and immediate. Most relationships begin with eros.
2. **Philia,** the second stage, represents the friendship that is formed after the initial attraction. This is when you form a deeper connection and begin to build a relationship upon the foundation of trust, companionship, fondness, and warmth. Philia tends to follow eros, but it can also stand alone, as in a platonic friendship.
3. As eros and philia continue to develop, **ludus**—the third stage—enters the scene. This is a playful kind of love that might involve flirting, teasing, and laughter. In my own case, Howard and I loved to dance together, and in the beginning, our dancing was fun and flirty—a clear expression of ludus. As our love deepened, the connection we felt while dancing transcended this stage and grew richer, deeper, and more intimate.

4. ***Agape*** is the fourth stage of love, and it involves selflessness and compassion. Agape is more active than some of the other stages, requiring the motivation to affect someone else—to make change. Without agape in a marriage, an imbalance can develop, as Howard and I would eventually find out.

5. ***Pragma,*** the fifth stage of love, exists when a deeper experience develops through compromise, patience, and tolerance. A strong marriage depends on pragma, which requires mutual commitment and long-term shared interests. Building a family together and supporting each other's career goals are examples of pragma.

6. Finally, ***philautia,*** the sixth stage, enters the picture. To experience philautia, one must overcome narcissism and develop a true capacity to love others selflessly. It requires understanding one's own worth and purpose and developing a sense of one's self in relation to others. As Aristotle reflected, "All friendly feelings for others are an extension of a man's feelings for himself."

It is likely that more has been written about love than about any other concept, and the word itself has taken on many connotations. The truth is, we tend to use it to mean whatever we want it to at the moment. That is why I find the definitions above to be so helpful. Breaking love down and thinking about each of these stages in turn, then exploring what they mean, how they progress, and how they might get bogged down, helped Howard and me figure out where we had thrived and where we had stumbled. In our case, the first three stages developed organically, while the last three were more of a challenge, and we had to put in some conscious effort to set them right.

As our story unfolds, perhaps you will discover ways in which you can use these six stages to think about your own relationships and unravel their mysteries.

Before we leave the topic of the six stages, I want to add that they can be applied to people in our lives other than our romantic partners. We all love a wide range of people, including friends, family members, work colleagues—and ourselves. An understanding of the six stages of love can be useful in all of these relationships and can help us navigate thorny moments and hold on to those who are precious to us. In this context, perhaps you will appreciate a comment made by the inspirational author Kate McGahan: "Just because someone doesn't love you the way you want them to doesn't mean they don't love you with all the love they have to give."

CHAPTER 3

WHY FAIRY TALES?

*"The heart of the fairy tale rests in its simplicity . . .
Victorians used this value of fairy tales to convey, in small
alchemical pictures, the path through the darkness . . ."*
—Max Lüthi, *The European Folktale: Form and Nature*

I have just told you that the creation of a happy marriage is not magic, so why am I taking you into the world of fairy tales, where magic abounds? Because they have so much to teach us about the subject.

Fairy tales, in their simplest reading and most obvious interpretation, portray both genders in a stereotypical manner. The ideal male is a savior, attractive, and courageous. The ideal woman is infinitely beautiful and in need of rescuing. If we look more deeply into these tales, however, there is much more to discover. In fact, there is alchemy, and as you make your way through this book, you will see where it exists. I will share how some very well-known fairy tales—such as *Cinderella* and *Hansel and Gretel*—as well as some lesser-known ones offer messages about how to safeguard a relationship and help it survive enormous psychological

11

and emotional challenges. I have chosen to connect fairy tales to our journey as a way to explore what "happily ever after" really means—and the toll it can take to achieve it.

We have already talked about gold as the ultimate prize in alchemy, but gold is an important element of fairy tales too. In stories, gold represents the most desirable element of all. In life, a happy marriage is our "gold standard." Is a good marriage—a "happily ever after"—an alchemical merging of elements, or is it a magical fairy tale? I believe it is both; I believe marriage is golden.

For hundreds of years, fairy tales have been cherished for their ability to transform a situation and, with a single decision, change the outcome of a life or a relationship. All our favorite fairy tales include elements of good and evil, light and dark—dichotomies that serve as metaphors for our own life journeys. Fairy tales clarify for us the paths we must choose as we move through our lives. They shed light on the nature of love and relationships, and offer hope for a satisfying ending.

The characters in fairy tales tend to end up stronger than they began, having surmounted whatever spells or magic—or simple misguided decisions—they experienced along their way.

Allow me to end these thoughts with a resonant quote from the marvelous storyteller Roald Dahl: "Above all, watch with glittering eyes the whole world around you because the greatest secrets are hidden in the most unlikely places. Those who don't believe in magic will never find it."

CHAPTER 4

DECISIONS BECOME CONCEPTS

"You are only one decision from a totally different life."

—Wilfred A. Peterson, American author

Over the course of our marriage, Howard and I came to understand the gravity of the decisions we made. We realized we would have to be willing to accept the consequences of those decisions. In looking back, I have developed some concepts related to the marriage journey, and I find them useful in understanding marriage in general. Perhaps they will be useful to you as well.

1. A marriage has a life of its own.

> "When I saw you, I fell in love, and you smiled because you knew."
>
> —Arrigo Boito, *Falstaff*

I remember the moment this thought entered my mind. It was while I was writing my previous book, *Moving Forward: The Widow's Journey*. As I gathered my thoughts about widowhood, it occurred to me that my book had taken on a life of its own. Originally, I had no intention of writing it, but several people who had supported me in my loss later prodded me to do so. Truth be told, I began writing about my experiences out of gratitude to them. Eventually, the book expanded to include the voices of thirteen other widows from diverse backgrounds and experiences, all of whom I interviewed extensively. The book, and the shape it eventually assumed, had not been in my life plan. It was as though it came to me and demanded I become its messenger.

At the point, when I realized the book had taken on a life of its own, I clearly remembered that I once had a similar thought twenty years earlier, during the most tumultuous time in my marriage. Back then, as I worked through the pain and challenges facing Howard and me, I came to the conclusion that my marriage had a life of its own—and that if we figured out how to protect it, life would prove stronger than either my husband or I were individually.

I wanted to include my thoughts about this in *Moving Forward,* but somehow, they just did not fit into the book I was writing. "This material might be the beginning of an entirely different book," noted my editor, and though neither of us realized it at the time, that was the seed of the book you are now reading.

As I thought more about the nature of marriage, several concepts took shape, but this central concept has remained the strongest and—I believe—the most useful idea of all and the one at the heart of this book.

As I prepared to write *The Alchemy of Love & Marriage*, I discussed the idea with four other people: a psychologist, an academic, and two avid readers. Interestingly enough, they all saw it somewhat differently. Each believed that the strength or weakness in a marriage lies strictly within the two individuals—that a marriage is only as strong as its parts. While I agree that two committed partners are integral to the success of any union, I remain convinced that the individuals are really just catalysts in service of a greater entity. I was happy to find validation in the words of the author and aviator Anne Morrow Lindbergh (wife of aviator Charles Lindbergh): "How hard is it to have the beautiful interdependence of marriage and yet be strong in oneself alone."

If, like a human cell, a marriage has its own life, then it must also have a nucleus in which elements of the two individuals are blended into something new. This new and essential thing is held together by love and designed to grow. Sometimes this new entity grows in a healthy way; sometimes it does not. One of the things Howard and I came to understand is that love, like life, is a developmental process. The road of life inevitably presents twists and turns, and in order to negotiate them, the marriage itself must be responsive—not just the two people within it.

The conflicts that arise in a marriage can be difficult to resolve. Sometimes resolution seems impossibly out of reach. Some people give up—and a number of them are right to give up. But when there is real value at the heart of a marriage and both individuals recognize this value and commit to safeguarding it, they may be able to find their way forward. In that effort, it is the unique life of the marriage itself that provides strength and safety, protecting the individuals from the storm of life raining down on them.

2. The whole of the marriage is greater than the sum of its parts.

> "It is not your love that sustains the marriage, but from now on, the marriage that sustains your love."
>
> —Dietrich Bonhoeffer, *Letters and Papers from Prison*

I am sure you have heard the saying, "The whole is greater than the sum of its parts." I believe it applies beautifully to marriage and is an obvious corollary to the first concept. Both of these concepts may seem simple, but the idea of applying them to marriage hit me like a thunderbolt, sizzling through my body from head to heart to soul. The force of these ideas was so strong that I actually had to stop in my tracks, sit down, and say to myself, "This marriage is an entity unto itself. It's stronger than either of us!" I only wish you could understand what an "Aha!" moment this was and how it reshaped my thinking about my life. It was a genuine turning point and a hopeful one.

As you will learn when you read our story, Howard suffered setbacks that made it impossible for us to keep moving forward together. If they had been left unaddressed, I feel certain our marriage could not have continued. Our nucleus was beginning to separate, and that could only mean death for the organism.

Thankfully, we (the parts) made a conscious effort to work together to save the whole, which I knew was the far greater entity. By understanding this, I came to regard its value as higher than that of Howard or myself. It was the most important thing in my life—our lives—and infinitely worth saving. This is not to say that we, the individuals, were not whole or important. I would not be here today, on my own, if that were the case. But, for as long as a marriage lasts, while the parts can only do their best to operate synchronously, the whole is the repository of strength and purpose.

3. Marriage is the third entity.

> "A healthy relationship is when two individual adults decide to have a relationship and that becomes a third entity. They nurture the relationship, and the relationship nurtures them. But they're not overly dependent or independent: They are interdependent, which means that they can take care of the majority of their needs and wants on their own, but when they can't, they're not afraid to ask their partner for help."
>
> —Neil Strauss, *The Truth: An Uncomfortable Book about Relationships*

I have already said this in various ways, but it is worth restating. Marriage is a third entity formed by two partners, and it requires nurturing and effort on the part of both individuals. You will see this at work in my own story, and you can probably identify it in yours.

While the marriage entity is not a physical being, like a man or a woman, it exists, composed of the thoughts, wants, needs, and actions of the two partners. In a marriage, these partners must maintain clear, constant, and honest communication in order for the third entity to remain intact. What can change, however, is the balance. Sometimes one individual is doing most of the emotional heavy lifting, and sometimes the other one is. These shifts are natural, and developing a rhythm for them is almost like learning to dance together. (As I have already mentioned, a love of dancing was at the emotional core of my relationship with Howard, so this is a particularly apt metaphor for us.) The ease of these shifts grows out of the couple's common purpose.

Aristotle wrote that genuine friends care more about each other's well-being than about their own—and that is certainly essential in a marriage. As life progresses to include jobs, children, travel, and all of life's many experiences, good and bad, this genuine selflessness—this love bond—becomes essential to navigating the world in tandem. Can you see now why I believe that, in marriage, one plus one can equal three?

To summarize the concepts that underpin the rest of this book: Marriage has a life of its own, becomes greater than the sum of its parts, and develops into its own entity. That said, I recognize that all marriages are different. As the years progressed, we recognized that our marriage had proved to be strong in order for us to move forward. We were also aware that occasionally there were situations when the fragility of the moment occurred, and we had to learn to walk together. In a crisis, we learned how to feed and nurture it as something separate from ourselves, and in the end, it healed, thrived, and deepened. And that became the greatest joy and reward of my life.

PART 2

THE STORY—WE ALL HAVE A STORY

"No story ever truly ends as long as it is told."

—Erin Morgenstern, *The Starless Sea*

A story takes you on a journey. If you are fortunate, reading it may lead you to experience wonder, learn to work through pain, and develop an appreciation for the conflicts challenging the characters. If the story captivates you, you may find yourself becoming one with it and experiencing your own growth and happiness. Stories pose questions, provide metaphors for life, and help us determine what transformations we must make in order to survive its challenges. Encountering the right story at the right time may help you explore who you are and how best to proceed along your own path.

I am sure you were taught that the best stories have a clear beginning, middle, and end. In the case of my marriage story, which I am about to recount, the beginning encompasses the early years of my marriage; the middle, our middle years; and the end, our later years. Naturally, challenges occur throughout, and changes become necessary. The characters (Howard and I) must confront the challenges and transform in response to them. Sometimes the challenges are minor or caused by external forces. But in one case, at least, our challenges were potentially shattering.

Welcome to our story; welcome to our journey.

CHAPTER 5

THE EARLY YEARS (HANSEL AND GRETEL GO INTO THE WOODS)

"The pain passes, but the beauty remains."

—Pierre-Auguste Renoir, French artist

A s is true for many couples, Howard's and my story began with intimacy. I can best express what I mean by *intimacy* by defining it as a combination of the first two of the Greeks' six stages of love, eros and philia. In case you need a reminder about these stages, it is eros that first possesses us, romantically and sexually. It is that bolt of attraction we have all felt, and it often takes hold quickly and without our consciously realizing it. Phila, the second stage, represents the friendship that usually is formed after the initial attraction. It adds a deeper connection to affinity, loyalty, and the beginning of trust.

We were married on a Sunday afternoon when I was twenty and Howard was twenty-one. We both worked while continuing our educations until we were about thirty. During that time, eros—intimacy and romance—dominated our physical existence. As F. Scott Fitzgerald expressed it in *This Side of Paradise*, "They slipped briskly into an intimacy from which they never recovered." We were quite fortunate about that. Yet, in a way, we were also like young Hansel and Gretel, going off into the woods and having to learn to survive.

We were young, inexperienced, and embarking on a journey without a map. If there was evil or difficulty ahead of us, we did not expect it, understand it, or plan for it. But we were together, a team, and that made us brave. We figured we could take care of each other—which is exactly what we set about doing.

To say we were a bit naïve is an understatement. In our early twenties, we had very little money, so we planned our European honeymoon with the help of a popular guidebook at the time, Arthur Frommer's *Europe on $5 a Day*. (Remember, there were no cell phones, no social media, and no websites to consult—and five dollars went a little further than it does today.) With help from Mr. Frommer, we booked the most economical overseas trip we could find: a thirteen-hour flight to Brussels on an Icelandic Airlines prop jet. Sadly, during this seemingly endless flight, my new husband caught some type of virus. He spent the full ten days we had arranged in Brussels sick in bed, leaving me pretty much on my own to explore a foreign country for the first time. (In fact, I had never been outside of New York City!)

Over those ten days, I earned the nickname "Rocky," after the Sylvester Stallone character who pushed himself against all odds and accomplished more than he could have imagined. I ventured from our hotel room to find food for Howard and soon learned that in 1968, shop owners in Brussels had never heard of "takeout." Shrugging, they referred me to hotel restaurants, where I cried and begged for sustenance for my new and very ill husband. Fortunately, I found the restaurant managers sympathetic and magnanimous. Some even gave me delicious hot meals on silver trays with real silverware, having no idea if they would ever see their property again. They simply knew I needed help and came to my aid.

Growing up in New York had afforded me some common-sense skills, but needing advice about specifics, I approached the staff of our hotel and asked, among other things, if they could recommend an English-speaking doctor. They did so and answered many other questions I had. I soon found myself walking along the tree-lined streets of Brussels alone, organizing my thoughts, following a paper map and the advice given to me, and taking baby steps forward each day.

The doctor came to the hotel, diagnosed Howard's virus, and recommended that he undergo a number of blood tests at a local hospital. Overcoming our trepidation about foreign medical care, we followed his instructions to the letter. My mission—taking care of my husband—gave me strength throughout the week, and we ultimately caught our grueling thirteen-hour flight home.

Howard's family doctor confirmed what we had learned in Brussels and validated the way we had handled it, and "Rocky" silently congratulated herself for passing her first test as a wife!

Two weeks later, although Howard was still a bit weak, we moved from New York City to Philadelphia to begin graduate school—Howard to dental school and I to study for my master's in education. To support ourselves, Howard worked part-time as a security guard, and I was a full-time teacher. As we walked into our new apartment, my new husband looked at me and said, "I feel better."

While I just shared with you the details of what may have been one of the worst honeymoons in history, I should note that it was indisputably a growth experience for me. Alone in Brussels, I was forced to grow up and take charge. This became part of the alchemy of our marriage—perhaps the first example of a process we would repeat over and over in different forms. I gave my all for Howard when he needed it, and he got better. On other occasions and in other ways, he would do the same for me. We were digging down to summon our best selves in support of our union and turning it into something more valuable than we could imagine. Looking back on that trip all these decades later, I can view it with humor and perspective. It was an ordeal and a trial by fire, but it was not just that; it was the beginning of a much larger experience and, in that way, exciting.

Having grown up in New York City, where public transportation is readily available and inexpensive, I had never learned to drive—but Philadelphia was a car town. It was Howard's turn to help me. For four years, he drove me to work each morning. After he completed his classes, he would study in the college library for hours, waiting for me to complete my evening classes. We were learning to get through our lives as a team.

Eventually, and with great patience, Howard taught me to drive. It would take me two tries to pass the driving test (a secret I rarely share), and when I did, we celebrated by sitting on a park bench with cupcakes—mine, chocolate, his, vanilla. We could not have been happier in that moment, two individuals supporting each other, cheering each other on, and moving forward together.

Passing my driving test was an exciting moment for me, and commemorating it ceremoniously made it eternally memorable. Sharing those cupcakes meant sitting close, slowing down, separating from the world while still appreciating our part in it. As we sat, we integrated the experiences that had led up to it (the many times we had practiced driving in the vacant parking lot of the Philadelphia Eagles stadium), the experience itself (taking the test not once, but twice), and the experiences to come (my future as an independent driver and a more independent woman). Through all of it, Howard was there with and for me; that was part of what we celebrated. Our precious time on the bench that day is present in my mind and heart even as I write this.

Park benches would come to figure prominently in our story. Over many years, we often found ourselves seated side by side on one in a quiet spot in nature, engaged in conversation. Sometimes these talks were lighthearted, loving, and pleasant; sometimes they were deeper, more difficult, and not so loving.

Thinking about it, I am struck by that iconic image of two figures side by side on a bench—talking, laughing, crying, or just sitting quietly. The simple act of resting in nature, connected to the ground, always helped us let go of stress and feel at peace, even when our interactions bordered on adversarial.

I believe that in those moments throughout our marriage when we would find ourselves on a park bench, our feet touching the verdant carpet below, we were experiencing the Japanese practice of forest bathing, drifting along together within a peaceful medium where we could engage deeply with ourselves, each other, and our surroundings. More often than not, we would find ourselves moving from confusion to calm in what I have come to see as just one more example—one more iteration—of the alchemy that occurs in marriage and makes it stronger.

At the beginning of our marriage, we related not just as lovers and friends but also in a fraternal way—as a brother and sister growing up together and finding our place in the larger world. The difference was that we did not have parental figures available for guidance, so we sometimes found ourselves forced to parent each other. Suddenly, we were expected to be leaders, constantly making decisions as we traveled an unfamiliar, sometimes frightening path.

It is easy to feel paralyzed in some situations, even with a partner. We came to realize, however, that there was great risk in *not* making decisions—even more risk than in making the wrong ones. While we recognized that we shared the dilemmas of many newly married couples, we often felt alone, as if in a deep forest on an untraveled road, like Hansel and Gretel. How could we keep from getting lost in the woods?

As I reflect on those first few years of our marriage, I recall that nothing was easy or ran smoothly. My mother-in-law was diagnosed with breast cancer shortly before we were married, and my brother discovered he had a muscle disease right afterward. These terrible events placed extreme pressure on us, and learning to deal with that pressure became a part of our development as a couple. We had to learn how to incorporate the ups and downs of family life into the exciting adventure of the newlywed experience.

My brother, Martin, with whom I am extremely close, had been my husband's best man at our wedding. When he told us of his devastating diagnosis, there was no question that Howard and I would be there to provide active support. This involved traveling back to northern New York from Philadelphia—a three-hour trip each way—nearly every weekend for the first year we were married. As we helped Martin, we shared the realization that the love of family would always be a priority for us and play a significant role in our lives. The honeymoon, good or bad, was over!

My time helping Martin through his muscle transplant surgeries and their aftermath entailed a lot of physical work. I would find myself on my knees, helping him put on his shoes and socks while Howard sat in a corner, studying for his advanced biology and chemistry courses, offering help when he could. On occasion, we would switch places: he, on the floor; I, attempting to study. Not surprisingly, we both experienced small flares of resentment.

After several weeks of juggling school, work, travel, and ministering to my brother, we were getting worn down. On our caregiving weekends, we would eat indifferently, then attempt sleep on separate air mattresses in the living room of a kind family friend who lived near the recuperation center. Needless to say, there was no romance during this period, no growing together, no becoming stronger as a couple. Months and months of this took its toll, unanticipated tensions developed, small arguments began, and outside pressure pierced our new nucleus of two.

I never believed, and still do not, that we had a transactional relationship. Ours was always a give-and-take experience without any desire to "keep score."

I believe those early challenges were typical of a new marriage. We were trying to do the right thing, but we were so young and inexperienced that, inevitably, small crevices developed as a result of our stresses. We did not have the wherewithal to address these at that time and felt that our bond—our intimacy—was strong enough to override them. Quite simply, life's possibilities seemed endless, and we felt strong enough to conquer anything. It was only with the passage of time and the onset of new and larger challenges that I came to understand the dangers inherent in leaving things unspoken.

I am happy to report that my extraordinary brother recovered, married, attained two master's degrees, and today still swims three days a week, walks long distances two days a week, and takes extensive bike trips with his wonderful children. Most recently, he danced the night away at his son's wedding. Not that I take any credit for it, but his is a remarkable "happily ever after."

On another note, if you knew our mother, you would understand that tenacity runs deep in both my brother and me! Throughout our childhood, long before Nike adopted it, Mom often invoked the phrase "Just do it." As my brother would attest, it was not said with warmth. Our eyes still roll when we reminisce about this firm familial goading. Is it always the right course to "just do it"? I am not sure, but she certainly was.

During our early years of marriage, Howard and I did experience things that brought us closer together—positive moments that helped balance out the stressful ones. One of them centered on an inanimate object: a wooden table. As I write this book in longhand, with pen and paper, I sit at the cherry-stained oak table I refer to. It is close to one hundred years old, and thinking about it gives me a feeling of breathing in sunshine. I remember how it came to us half a century ago and the many hours I have spent sitting at it since. Writing at this table is integral to my creative process. Its generous size enables me to move my many yellow handwritten pages around as my thoughts grow into sentences, paragraphs, and, eventually, stories. It was while working at this table that I recognized my passion for writing, and it is where my creative growth takes place.

The table came to us from a kind friend in Philadelphia in 1968, our first year of marriage. While in her possession, it had become damaged, and as she was unable to repair it, she gave it to us.

Howard had refinished some old oak pieces during our senior year in college so we would have some furniture for our first apartment, and he was delighted at the prospect of a reclamation project. He spent the next three months repairing, sanding, staining, and oiling the table while I helped as best I could. I did not realize it at the time, but that tandem effort would produce a physical object of great importance to our life together. We were becoming our own alchemists.

The table, which we both considered beautiful as well as useful, was where I studied for my degrees. It was where our children did their homework and where we gathered for family dinners every night for a quarter century. And today, here I sit, bent over its burnished top as I search for the words to tell my story.

As a side note, I have recently listened to interviews with two people much more successful and famous than I: the philanthropist and entrepreneur David Rubenstein and Christine Lagarde, who headed the International Monetary Fund and the European Central Bank. I was fascinated to learn that they, too, have made a tradition of working at their dining tables. And the "table club" has at least one more member as well. According to one of his biographers, Michael Katakis, Ernest Hemingway wrote a good part of his first published novel, *The Sun Also Rises,* on a large table in Spain. "I wrote in great luxury on the table," Hemingway commented. So, I find myself in grand company as I write this book for you.

There were other objects that came to us in those years that helped provide balance for the more difficult moments to come.

One was a stained-glass *Welcome* sign. During our second year in Philadelphia, we enjoyed taking day trips to towns and hamlets outside the city, stopping for nice lunches along the way. On one of those drives, we stopped in a local shop and saw a beautiful glass sign in pastel colors featuring the word *Welcome* in bright red. It was encased in wood, and the lights behind it made it glow invitingly. After staring at it for a while, we asked the shopkeeper about it, and he told us about the art of stained glass and the gentleman who had made it.

Howard decided on the spot that he could recreate the sign and went on to spend well over a year of his spare time working on it. First, he sketched a pattern on brown paper, then consulted a few stained-glass artisans. Per their instructions, he purchased colorful glass, learned how to cut it and solder it together, and eventually, the sign took shape. To say this was an amateur production is putting it mildly, but it was his best effort, and the sign became a cherished object in our lives. Like the wood table, the sign traveled with us to every place we lived and hangs high in my kitchen now, lighting up each night.

What had begun in our early years as an effort to hand-make something beautiful became a lasting symbol of our development as a couple. Today, Howard is gone, and I have had to learn to move forward without him. (This difficult yet ultimately rewarding process is central to my previous book, *Moving Forward: The Widow's Journey*). The oak table, the *Welcome* sign, these are a couple of the reasons I continue to live in the home we shared. Howard may live on only in memory, but these objects are here. They are the tangible evidence of a lifelong bond and remind me that Howard will always be with me.

It is important for me to talk about the challenges we faced in those early years. In addition to helping my brother through his illness, we moved three different times over the next nine years. We both continued to work and go to school, and we welcomed two children into the world. How we juggled all of it, I have absolutely no idea, but we did. We just kept trying to move ahead together. Possibly, we were too busy facing whatever came along to stop! Or maybe we were just too inexperienced to know that a pause for reflection could renew our strength. We did occasionally take a breath, share a meal, smile at each other, and then get back to it. We were together, and that was all that mattered to us. It helped immeasurably as we walked hand in hand into those dark woods.

Our move to Philadelphia just after we got married was our first out-of-state move, and I have already shared with you some of the changes it brought. When I told friends about our plans, they just stared at me. "Where will you shop?" one of them asked. "Do you think you will be able to find a job?" I reassured them that with my teaching degree, job opportunities would be plentiful. Philadelphia at the time was, after all, the fourth-largest city in the US, and, while not New York, it offered everything we could possibly need.

We moved into the most inexpensive apartment we could find, which happened to be in West Philadelphia—not the safest place in 1968. I earned $6,000 a year teaching third and fourth grade in a public school that boasted the lowest academic scores in the district. At night, I attended classes in literature, history, philosophy, and education that did not end until 10:00 p.m. On weekends, we cleaned the apartment and studied.

Howard had wonderful older cousins with a sixth sense for inviting us to dinner just when we were absolutely spent and needed it most. As much as the dinners and other kindnesses helped us move through the arduous days and weeks, we were being affected by our trials in ways we did not even realize. If anyone had asked us how we were doing at the time, I am sure we both would have answered, "Just fine."

Our next move was to Morgantown, West Virginia, where my husband completed a US Public Health Service obligation, and I attended West Virginia University on a doctoral fellowship. I could hardly believe my meager stipend—just $2,500 a year, for which I taught two undergraduate classes and took on whatever else I was asked to do. It was a poverty-level wage, but the free tuition was a godsend.

The students in my two classes were all women, all born and raised in West Virginia and all intending to become teachers while their male counterparts prepared to go to work in the coal mines. Miners' pay was the highest of any profession in the state, and the work did not require a degree. These young men were aware of the dangers of mining and the risk of developing black lung disease, but they simply had no better options.

One morning, when I arrived for my 8:00 a.m. class, all twenty students were sitting in a circle waiting for me. This took me aback, as I usually arrived first. One of the girls explained that they had a group request. "We know you're from New York City," she said, "and none of us has ever left West Virginia. We want to see New York—and we want you to take us there."

I just stared.

"We'll save up the money we need for food and stuff," she continued in a rush of words. "We've got it all planned! We'll drive there in four different cars, one following another. And when we get there, we'll follow you to wherever you want to take us."

I was stunned and sat silently for a moment while their eager faces fell. Not wanting to hurt their feelings, I said, "I'm surprised, and . . . flattered . . . but I have no idea how to make this happen."

They sat quietly.

Could I actually do this?

"Here is what I do know," I slowly continued. "You will need three days plus a weekend."

Their faces perked up again.

"I may be asked to sign you out of classes, and I'll navigate that as best I can. If we pull this off, you'll all have to sleep at my mother-in-law's house in Brooklyn—on the floor of her basement—so bring a sleeping bag. We'll travel around the city by subway, doing whatever sightseeing I can think of, and I'll also find a school for you to visit in order to justify the 'educational' nature of the trip. I'll try to arrange for us to see a show, visit a museum, and walk through a variety of neighborhoods. As for the food, well . . . it'll have to be cheap, but there's lots of good cheap food in New York."

By this time, the girls were beaming.

"So," I said, catching a bit of their enthusiasm, "assuming I can make it happen, I guess we're off on an adventure!"

Just imagine my poor husband's face when I shared the prospect of the field trip with him that evening. Even better, imagine my mother-in-law's face when I called her with the news. Finally, imagine the face of the college dean when he called me into his office several days later to discuss the student permission forms that would require my signature as well as those of the students' other professors.

"Who are you?" he demanded point-blank. "And exactly what do you think you're up to?"

Somehow I produced a satisfactory answer, and off we went. Word had spread throughout Morgantown about our caravan and intention to "camp" in a Brooklyn basement. Our adventures included riding subways, enjoying a show at Radio City Music Hall, visiting the Metropolitan Museum of Art, eating at an array of diners and street carts, and—of course—the obligatory visit to a public school in Queens. Everyone was on her own our last morning, with plans to meet up at noon. As you can imagine, my heart skipped many beats until all the girls were present and accounted for. Being responsible for their well-being made the trip as much an adventure for me as it was for them.

We all returned to West Virginia intact, bonded, and with lots of stories to tell.

My time in West Virginia proved important not only for me as an educator but also for Howard and me as a couple. We both gained important work and life experience and managed to enjoy ourselves as well.

Howard fulfilled his military obligation by working for the Department of Prisons in a minimum-security facility for young people. The inmates had to return to their quarters at 4:00 p.m., leaving him an hour and a half of free time each day to complete his paperwork and reflect on the work he was doing.

We did not have children yet, so Howard had time to enjoy his hobbies in the evening while I studied. These included exercising and refurbishing any worthy piece of oak furniture he thought might be a nice addition to our home. When we both had free time, we would scout secondhand furniture shops for these pieces, at one point finding the perfect rolltop desk just begging for Howard's efforts. He would spend two years of spare hours bringing it back to life—finally applying the same cherry oak stain he had used on the dining table so we would have matching pieces. I still have that beautiful desk at which Howard worked for the rest of his life.

In thinking back on our two years in Morgantown, I recall the peace we felt there after our tumultuous four years in Philadelphia. We had a little bit of money, a little extra time, a few adventures (I attended an ox roast!), and a sense that we were growing together and working toward our future. While there were still occasional challenges—we were not out of those dark woods yet, after all—there were many moments when the sunshine broke through the trees and we experienced tranquility.

Our last move during that nine-year "beginning" period of our marriage was back to Philadelphia for three more years so that Howard could complete an orthodontic program. For my part, I served as an adjunct professor at several universities. Those years were also taken up with the excitement and joy of having two healthy babies, along with the new responsibilities that entailed. We were grown-ups now, and there was no turning back! As we completed our formal educations, we would have to decide where to begin our adult lives and how to sustain our family of four.

We left Philadelphia with no debt but no savings either. Not knowing exactly what our next chapter would hold, we found ourselves still lost in the woods.

CHAPTER 6

REFLECTIONS AND THOUGHTS ON THE EARLY YEARS

*"The future belongs to those who believe
in the beauty of their dreams."*

—Eleanor Roosevelt, First Lady and humanitarian

I have used the metaphor of Hansel and Gretel to convey not only our youth and inexperience but also our ability to clasp hands as we entered the unknown and worked together to survive. Sometimes Howard would provide reassurance when I was apprehensive, and sometimes it would be my turn to do that for him.

If you recall the fairy tale, it is Hansel who comes up with the idea of scattering pebbles as they walk so that they might find their way back home. "Be comforted, dear little sister," he says, just as Howard would sometimes tell me to trust that a plan he had would work. And when, on their second attempt to create a pathway back home, they scatter breadcrumbs that are gobbled up by birds, they survive because they still have each other. Howard and I had a few failures along the way as well, but we found our strength by sticking together.

Ultimately, Hansel and Gretel encounter an evil witch who lures them into a cottage made of delicious treats and then imprisons Hansel in a stable. What can Gretel do but develop a new plan? She figures out a way to distract the witch and free her brother so that they can vanquish their enemy forever.

Within the magical environment of the tale, Hansel and Gretel transform from fearful children into confident, competent people. Taking turns at the forefront and working together when they can, they move from darkness into light, enslavement into freedom. They survive because the entity they create together is greater and stronger than its constituent parts. They create a third entity—and that is the agent of their triumph.

Like Hansel and Gretel, Howard and I recognized early on that our best bet in facing our challenges was to combine forces and come up with a joint plan. Our marriage story offers evidence of our personal and mutual transformation—the alchemy that can occur when two people commit to working together. Of course, no couple does all this alone. We had help from others along the way and—like Hansel and Gretel—sometimes even the benefit of a little magic.

In comparing our story to a fairy tale, I have asked you to use your imagination. That is something I find essential in understanding the connection of real life to fairy tales, as well as the role of alchemy in marriage. Perhaps you will have to take it on faith, but I believe that the greater your imagination, the more powerful your outcome.

By understanding the implications of fairy tales and adapting the actions of their characters to your own life, you are tapping into the power of enchantment to create transformation. The idea is to connect magic and logic. If you can find a balance by bringing a higher level of logic to a relationship without diluting the magic as life changes, you can still dream. As for alchemy, its principles are embedded in those tales, which embody its message: the base material of two lives, when combined with the magic of love, can result in the most valuable, unimaginable result.

In closing out this section about our early years, I want to offer a few concluding thoughts. Throughout our time in Philadelphia, Morgantown, and then Philadelphia again, our focus was on work and school (and, at the end, our children). Although we had very little money, we never dwelt on it. Our focus was clear, and we were directed, but we never stopped dancing—always dancing.

In retrospect, I think of the whole first decade of our marriage as the "early years." I am aware that in addition to the various stages of love we traversed, a lot of it was about education, work, and money—yet eros, philia, and especially ludus always prevailed. As Howard and I danced through those early years, we sometimes executed a perfect tango but more often stepped on each other's toes. As we entered the stage called agape, our friendship and trust were blossoming and served to strengthen our love's foundation.

The passion of eros does not have to dissipate as philia develops. As we dated, then married, then navigated married life, the trust and the sharing between us took hold without pushing eros to the side. We never confused the two, and we appreciated both as fully as we could. Writing in the eighteenth century, Samuel Taylor Coleridge put it perfectly when he noted, "Friendship satisfies the highest parts of our nature, but a [beloved], who is capable of friendship, satisfies all."

CHAPTER 7

THE MIDDLE YEARS (HANSEL AND GRETEL MEET THE WITCH)

"Sometimes the things we think are lost are only hidden, waiting to be rediscovered."

—Anthony Doerr, *Cloud Cuckoo Land*

Having fully experienced the Greeks' first two stages of love—eros and philia—during our early years, we moved into our middle period, and the next two stages came into play: ludus and agape.

Ludus, as you will recall, is the playful, flirty stage, which we both found extremely enjoyable. We were dancing more than ever! This aspect of our love would remain strong throughout our life together as our feelings of friendship and trust steadily grew. There is nothing superficial about ludus; in fact, it runs very deep. To illustrate, as the American author Hua Hsu remarked in his memoir *Stay True*, "Some friends complete us, while others complicate us."

Agape, the fourth stage, focuses on selfless love and compassion—putting your mate's needs and desires ahead of your own. This does not necessarily develop naturally, and in our case, it took quite a while to take hold—not that we fully recognized this at the time. Albert Einstein famously said, "Only a life lived for others is a life worthwhile," but this is more easily said than done, and I have to wonder if Einstein himself lived up to it. The empathy that agape requires was not in full enough supply in our marriage, and this created a crevice. Mind you, not even the people closest to us were able to spot it, but Howard and I could feel—if not name—the formation of the rift. We could only hope that over time we would be able to repair it. No two people live in lockstep, and every marriage has its own timetable. Often, one party moves ahead of the other, only to find the positions reversed later on.

Over a decade and three moves, we completed our education and professional preparation. We also expanded our family nucleus from two to four. As I previously noted, we were grown-ups now.

We chose Miami, Florida—a place of growth and opportunity for a family such as ours—to begin the next part of our journey through what I think of now as our middle years. It seemed an appealing city with great diversity, several universities, and a relaxed lifestyle, so off we went from Philadelphia with our three-week-old and two-year-old in tow. As with many moves, not everything went smoothly, but in about three weeks, we found ourselves settled into an apartment building that even boasted a pool.

Howard had a job, and I had a variety of opportunities at local universities. In 1977, there was not a plethora of women with doctorates, so I found myself in the right place at the right time.

A year after relocating, we had adjusted to our new jobs and family responsibilities and decided it was time for Howard to set up his own orthodontic practice. This involved obtaining a business loan, about which we really knew nothing. However, like Cinderella, we found our own "fairy godmother."

We started by walking into our local bank. A lovely woman asked us some general questions about our education, work, and assets, then asked how much we thought we would need. Howard responded, and she followed up by asking about our collateral.

We just looked at each other.

"Do you own cars?" she asked, and we were excited to say that we did—a twenty-one-year-old and a fifteen-year-old.

"Do you own a home or property?"

"Well . . . no," we had to admit.

Things proceeded in this manner until the woman said she had to confer with her vice president. Within twenty minutes, she returned and said she was sorry, but we did not meet the bank's criteria for a loan.

We looked at each other and touched hands, our minds racing about where we would turn next.

"But," she continued, "that doesn't seem right to me. I explained to our vice president that you are extraordinary people who have accomplished a tremendous amount through your own hard work and perseverance. 'These people aren't a risk,' I said. 'They are an investment.'"

She was our fairy godmother. You cannot imagine how excited we were at the thought of going into debt!

Every month for five years, we walked into that bank with a cup of coffee for our friend and made our monthly loan payment.

The day we made our last payment, she took us to lunch—as modern-day fairy godmothers do!

Over time, our challenges were many. We continued to build our life together as couples do, raising our children and buying a house. We were not particularly prepared for either activity, but the house proved particularly difficult because it was falling apart when we acquired it. It was not so much that we had made a poor choice as a necessary one: no down payment was required for this particular property, rendering it the practical option—or so it seemed.

Throughout our thirties and mid-forties, we flirted, trusted, and enjoyed our life together. As our mutual trust grew, we took more risks and frequently teased each other. We often found ourselves literally dancing around the house, moving together as a unit. Sometimes, when we were on different floors, working or studying separately, Howard would call down to me, "Arlene, come up here quickly," which I always did. I would find him listening to a favorite piece of music (how he could work and listen at the same time I will never understand), and when I arrived in the doorway, he would stand, smile, and reach out his hands. Into his arms I would go, and we would dance for a moment or two. Sometimes we would enjoy a quickstep, laughing as we moved, while other times, it would be a slow dance that would send a frisson of eros through our veins. When the music ended, I would go back downstairs and resume my studies, and Howard would return to his work. It was just a moment in our day, but what a sustaining moment!

Dancing serves as a good analogy for navigating a marriage. In each endeavor, two people must work together to move smoothly. One usually leads while the other follows, but the active cooperation of both parties is required. And when it is done well, it appears effortless, even while great effort is being expended by both partners. Finally, a well-executed dance elicits joy from both the participants and those around them. If that does not sound like a good marriage, I do not know what does.

I like to think that Howard and I brought the same qualities to our marriage as those that made us successful on the dance floor, and this helped us manage the challenges that came our way. There are times when spouses evolve together, and those are marvelous times. Other times, it can feel as though you are going in completely different directions, and that can be unsettling.

As we began to make friends with other young families and put down roots in our community, nothing was overwhelmingly difficult, but nothing was easy either. We fell into roles that might be called "traditional" by today's standards, but we never saw this as a choice; we simply knew no other way.

We were still Hansel and Gretel, walking deeper into the forest, but now it was time to meet the witch. In our case, that had to do with adjusting to life in suburbia.

As lifelong city dwellers, Howard and I had both grown up "on the block," products not just of our nuclear families but also of our neighborhoods. I had come of age in an apartment building and Howard in a small row house—in close-knit communities that provided a particularly rich level of socialization. We had interacted constantly with the families around us and learned how to be individuals within what might otherwise be considered too large a group. This was because we were raised based on the belief that everyone in a community, regardless of the size of the group, has a voice. It was our responsibility to honor each other. On the block, no one was born special. Leadership transitioned from one person to another as situations changed, and we were judged by what we were good at, whether it was schoolwork or stickball.

Many of us would gather after school (usually divided up by gender) to blow off steam before dinner and homework. We had to learn to assert ourselves and make our voices heard. One person in the group—someone different each day—would select the afternoon's activity, and the rest of us would go along with that choice.

Here, I would like to share a childhood story of mine about a girl named Shelly, who moved with her mother into my building from a small farm in upstate New York after her dad passed away. Of course, I asked her to join our rather large after-school group. Eventually, it was Shelly's turn to assume leadership of the group and choose an activity.

Although she was friendly enough, Shelly seemed a bit odd to us. "I would like us all to play gods and goddesses on Mount Olympus," she declared, then chose a few of us to climb a small hill. The others were to play the parts of mortals and gather below. This was a new kind of game for us, but after a moment or two, we followed her instructions and spent a memorable afternoon learning from our new friend about the intricacies of Greek mythology.

Shelly later transferred to a school for gifted children, but most afternoons, she made it home in time to play with the rest of us. Respectfully accepting one another's differences was thus ingrained in us from an early age, and I maintain that I am the better for it to this day.

Looking back, I have no idea how we managed to so seamlessly take turns being leader, but we did—and it proved to be great preparation for life. Our roles were neither restrictive nor permanent. Our goal was to work together and have fun, and we did it without ever having been taught how.

As we transitioned from childhood to young adulthood, we became more aware of the world around us and its demands and benefits. Here is an example: When Howard and I were around nineteen and dating, we decided to take a stroll through Central Park one day on our way to dinner. It was about 5:00 p.m., the air was cool, and the sky was blue as we passed a fenced-in field where a group of young men were playing softball. To our surprise, one of the guys ran over to us and spoke to Howard through the fence.

"Hey, buddy!" he said. "We're a man short. Can you play?"

I am sure Howard would have loved to join them; he was a Brooklyn boy, after all. But we were on a schedule, and he certainly was not dressed for an impromptu game.

"Sorry," he said sincerely, "but I'm on my way across town with my girl here."

I observed the motley assortment of players and found myself smiling. They were not wearing any kind of uniform—not even caps—and they varied in age, size, and economic background. Clearly, nobody cared about any of those superficial differences; they were just there to have fun playing a game they all loved. This was city life. At that moment, they were short a man, and Howard would have fit in just fine. We had moved beyond the block, but the city was an extension of it. We were still, and without effort, part of a community.

Perhaps you can understand, then, why our "exile" to suburbia involved a genuine adjustment for both of us. That element of community where strangers become family quite naturally was something we both missed desperately. In retrospect, I believe that had an impact on our relationship over the years.

It is not that we spent a lot of time questioning or regretting our choice. We had chosen to spend our middle years in the suburbs for very good reasons. In addition to the affordability of the real estate, there was our proximity to work, the quality of the schools, and the prospect of having the indoor and outdoor space we needed. Plus, we were surrounded by other young families, and there were lots of activities for children. That is suburbia in a nutshell, and it certainly seemed positive. But as time progressed, our city selves fought back against our surroundings, sometimes to the point of creating overt tension. Quite simply, we felt trapped.

We had to admit to ourselves and each other that suburbia was a place where we would never quite fit in, no matter how hard we tried. Why this was, we could not say. Why could we not find happiness in a place where everything is planned and regulated? After-school activities were scrupulously organized, and children were closely monitored. Parents were expected to participate, help coordinate, and intervene when necessary. Lots of people who had come from large cities, as we had, found this all quite appealing. We figured we would too, until we lived there.

We considered our options and, for whatever reason, decided it would be best to live with our mistake and plod along like good soldiers. In retrospect, we were probably afraid of making yet another mistake. The consequence of toughing it out was an added stress on our marriage that escalated over time and nearly cost us all that we cherished.

Once we had reconciled ourselves to it, our lives proceeded in an orderly fashion. Saturday-night dinners within various social groups were the norm, and everyone was expected to take a turn in hosting them. This proved burdensome for Howard and me since we both worked at least part of every Saturday. The reality for us was that we did not have a lot of time for adult socializing on *any* day of the week. We worked long hours, and any free time we had was reserved for family activities.

This set us apart from most of our neighbors. Suburban women did not tend to work outside the home in the late '70s and early '80s, and my neighbors found it hard to understand our situation. Why on earth would we choose pizza night with our children or Sunday bagels at home over a civilized social event with our peers? This disjunction made us feel like misfits in our own neighborhood—as if we were trying to retain our city customs in the suburbs, and it just was not working. We had assumed that suburbia was the "right" place to raise our family, without fully reflecting on our specific tastes, values, and goals. At the time, it was easier to adhere to social norms and expectations than to forge a unique path.

Our witch's cottage in the forest was suburbia itself, a beautiful and tempting trap that proved perilous for our relationship.

The crack that formed as a result was growing without our awareness of the implications.

Another massive challenge of those years involved the larger world and our place in it. This was a time of enormous social change, and navigating it proved tricky for many couples, including us. The '60s and '70s brought the civil rights movement, the Vietnam War, the rise of feminism, and Watergate. Many marriages based on strong mutual affinities were suddenly forced to face differences that threatened to tear them apart. Learning to communicate across rifts caused by gender roles and politics led many couples to question whether they belonged together at all. Some decided to move on separately, and divorce became more common and less stigmatized.

As I reflect back on that period, my views may sound naïve or just old-fashioned, but keep in mind that I was very much a product of my upbringing. Yes, I was working outside the home—something considered "progressive" at the time. But when it came to my marriage and those of women like me, the expectations remained relatively unchanged from what they had been in the '50s. Wives were expected to fulfill their traditional responsibilities in support of their husbands, households, and children. More and more women were joining the workforce, but the man was still the head of the house, still catered to, still cooked for. Women's work in the home became what social psychologist Arlie Hochschild termed their "second shift," creating a serious imbalance and the turmoil that goes with it.

Howard and I were navigating this imbalance without even realizing it. Although we had both gone to college and graduate school, we operated under the assumption that *his* career came first. Certainly, there was more social pressure on Howard to be successful professionally, but I was expected to do my job well *and* act as primary caregiver, homemaker, and social planner. While celebrating the social change that had elevated women's roles in the workforce, we were leaving the consequences to our home life unexamined.

Like most men, Howard was content with the situation. Why would he not be? While the economic aspect of our life improved because of my paycheck, he took on no new responsibilities. Women's needs just were not part of the equation in most marriages, and ours was no different. We carried on without noticing that yet more cracks were forming in the foundation of our life together.

Having children was, of course, the norm, and while everyone tells you your life is about to change, no one really explains the challenges children can impose on a marriage. Once your beautiful baby comes home, the reality of its complete dependence on you for every little thing hits like a ton of bricks. The nucleus of two, your marriage, has expanded and changed, and there is no going back. And again, the bulk of the burden of rearing that child falls on one party—usually, and in our case, the mother— and that imbalance takes its toll. Our lives and marriage had simply seemed easier to balance when there existed just two of us. (Picture two people on a seesaw, placidly bouncing up and down in turn. Now add another unruly person or two, and imagine how hard it is to keep everything balanced and pleasurable!)

At any point in a marriage, there are variables and unexpected turns. Perhaps one of you loses your job or gets sick. But children compound these variables; it seems something unforeseen is always happening within the family. And, of course, the amount of money you need to live well escalates dramatically. These things affect the alchemy of the marriage you have so carefully constructed. Your life is constantly thrown into chaos, and you are forced to navigate together as best you can. It is as if the alchemist's assistant waltzed into the room and knocked some unknown substance into your previously well-mixed formula. How can you ensure that you will still end up with gold? In our case, Howard and I did the best we could to keep our mixture pure, all the while hoping and praying the gold would appear. It involved making choices unrelated to our ultimate quest for the "happily ever after."

The stress children add to a marriage does not end as they grow out of babyhood. I remember a period during our children's preteen years when Howard and I had an argument they overheard. I am not talking about a brief spat but a prolonged one that took place over three days.

On the third night, at about 2:00 a.m., I could hear my daughter, Mara, down in the kitchen. I found her drinking Pepto-Bismol directly from the bottle, a telltale pink mustache decorating her upper lip.

"What on earth are you doing, Mara?" I asked her, aghast.

"I just can't stand you and Daddy arguing," she responded through tears. *"I . . . I . . . just can't take it!"*

"Oh, sweetheart," I said, embracing her in a hug. "I'm so sorry. So is Daddy. Do not worry about it; everything will be fine in the morning."

When I finally got a smile out of her by showing her how funny she looked with her pink upper lip, she let me walk her back up to her room, where she climbed into bed. After gently closing her door, I went back to my own room, woke up Howard, and told him what had transpired.

"Oh no," he sighed. He could never stand to see either of our children in pain.

"This argument ends now, whatever our differences," I declared. "We can sort things out without dragging the children into it. Honestly, at this point, I don't care which one of us gets our way."

"Neither do I," he replied.

We both recognized that the health and well-being of our children were more important than whatever we were fighting about. (I honestly cannot even remember what it was.) We were absolutely moving together on this one. Children may bring stress to a marriage, but in this instance, they led us back onto our true path. We fell back to sleep holding hands, and in the morning, went out to a local café for breakfast and a productive conversation.

Today, partners in a marriage tend to talk about things openly, and if they do not have the language to do so, they often consult a therapist or counselor. In our day, we simply did not talk about things—or, at least, not until they got very serious. We were expected to figure out how to negotiate life's changes and challenges almost by magic. And by challenges, I mean everything from disciplining the children to making ends meet. We just held on as tightly as we could and faced each day.

Over time, I have come to understand that breaking out of the rigid roles Howard and I were expected to follow was for the best. Couples today are much better equipped to face the realities of marriage than we were—but these changes came a bit late for us. Based on our own backgrounds and upbringings, we were ill-equipped to process the vast social changes that came about during our middle years. Unlike our children, we had no role models for how best to juggle parenthood and professional life.

This was especially true for women of the time. Men of the next generation would learn to take on a greater share of the parenting and household responsibilities and move toward a new paradigm. These sea changes have continued to evolve to this day. What is clear from conversations I have had with women a decade or two (or three) younger than I is that the situation is better but still far from perfect.

To be fair to Howard, he was not unresponsive to change. Over time, he began to take on a greater role at home, assisting with chores and actively helping me manage our domestic life. In fact, I think he took to these new responsibilities more naturally than many men did at that time. He fell madly in love with each of our newborns in turn and took great joy in playing an active role in their lives.

Were we doing all right in those years? In some ways, yes. We were carrying on with a minimum of conflict, and I think we were both grateful for the marriage we had, especially when we looked around at some others we knew. But those cracks and stresses remained unattended and were consequently growing more severe and dangerous.

I think it is important to note that even when we made a decision based on Howard's needs, it often proved positive for me as well. The next move we made is the best example of this.

We relocated to Miami, Florida, in July 1977—admittedly not the best time to go south. We were greeted by heat, humidity, and storms we Northerners were ill-prepared to tolerate.

Howard found himself more disappointed in our choice than I did. He missed a temperate climate and changing seasons, his extended family, and his friends and colleagues. For my part, I was too busy to be disappointed and hoped he would settle in.

After two years, Howard's attitude had not gotten much better, and I decided we needed to plan something—even if small—to bring fun back into our lives. We agreed that a vacation was in order, just the two of us, one week a year—no matter what.

I wanted Howard to decide where we should go since he was more in need of a getaway than I was. We had always enjoyed bicycling, so he chose a group bike trip with Vermont Bicycle Touring. The idea was that we would explore a different area each spring, and we eagerly awaited our first trip to the "Green Mountain State."

The trip did provide a much-needed break for Howard from the "hamster wheel" he felt he was on. As he had always been an athlete, he enjoyed the biking a lot more than I did and had much greater endurance. I left the strenuous rides to him and took some of the shorter routes, and I secretly enjoyed jumping on the accompanying van in the afternoons, which stopped for homemade ice cream. We both found our slice of enjoyment and freedom on those trips and stuck to our plan to repeat them annually.

On one of them, I decided to join the larger group at the end of the last day. This group had traveled the curved paths, so they had ridden an average of twenty-five miles per day, compared with our eight or ten. As the two groups converged to make our way down the last hill together, I sailed along, smiling broadly and feeling absolutely at one with nature. In my state of bliss, I failed to notice a professional photographer on the side of the road, taking pictures for the company's upcoming posters and brochures. Guess who ended up as an official cover girl the following winter? When the poster and brochure arrived in the mail, Howard looked at me and said, "I can't believe it! You joined our group on the last day, and you're on the cover!" "I did it for you," I insisted, and we had a good laugh about it. I could not resist framing the images, and they still hang on my upstairs wall, alongside other family photos.

Since this anecdote reflects positively on me, it is only fair that I share one that is favorable to Howard. On another bike trip, a drizzly one also in the fall—this time, in North Carolina—our group consisted of eight adults and two children aged ten and twelve. I remember mentioning to Howard that we had never been on a bike trip that permitted children and that the rain might make the downhill parts particularly perilous for them. "Those kids are here with their parents," he reminded me. "I guess that's *their* problem."

The fourth day of the trip included a long downhill stretch over slippery leaf-strewn roads. As Howard was the stronger rider, he moved ahead with the two children and their father while I stayed back with the slower group. Sure enough, the twelve-year-old girl lost control of her bike, went flying, and landed face down.

The van that accompanied us pulled over and an ambulance was called, but Howard insisted on examining her mouth. To his horror, he noted that her braces and teeth had attached to the roof of her mouth. The dentist had to be very skilled in this type of surgery as this could cause permanent disfigurement if not dealt with precisely.

When the ambulance arrived, the driver told Howard that the girl would be taken to the local hospital, where she would be attended to by a general surgeon.

"Absolutely not!" Howard bellowed. "Her face has been distorted by this crash, and she must be treated by a plastic surgeon and an oral surgeon! I will take care of repairing her braces and moving her teeth back immediately, but I insist: If these specialists are not available, find some and fly them in!"

The EMS workers looked at my husband, clearly unhappy with his directives.

"Do what Dr. Sacks says!" shouted the girl's father.

Howard and the surgeons worked through the night, and when he returned the next afternoon, he was spent but pleased. Clearly, the stars were aligned for this girl. What were the chances that a trained and assertive orthodontist from Miami would take charge of her care in a small town in North Carolina?

Not only did the story have a happy ending, but the girl's parents were kind enough to keep us informed over the years. Their pretty daughter grew up with no scars and went on to live a happy life.

Although I stated early on in this book that our story had no heroes, this was a genuinely heroic moment for Howard, and his actions provided a "happily ever after" for a young girl we had met by chance. Real life may have its cracks and crevices, but it has heroic moments as well.

Vacations are wonderful, but they end. Back in our real lives, the little stresses and strains persisted. I continued to be the primary caregiver while Howard served as the primary breadwinner, and it fell to me to adapt and solve any problems that arose. I did the best I could, but somehow Howard was still the one who felt the stress most keenly, and it began to overwhelm him. A crack was deepening, and, looking back, I realize that I was too busy to acknowledge that there might be consequences.

As the next few years passed, Howard gradually withdrew from me. While he continued to give his all to our children and never seemed angry, he just was not as present for me as he had once been, and our sense of intimacy eroded. I brushed this aside and focused on the two small people who depended on us. I could not or did not want to see that my husband was falling down a rabbit hole, and there was no one there to drop down a ladder.

Things might have continued to deteriorate unexamined had we not embarked on a much-needed and eagerly anticipated family vacation. Relatives had generously offered us a two-week stay at their beautiful cabin in Dillon, Colorado, with views of the Rocky Mountains. We packed our bags and headed off, eager to introduce our children to the glorious West and the kinds of outdoor activities we loved.

We found ourselves in a beautiful new place, but we had brought our troubles along for the ride. Unburdened by work and household responsibilities, we had hoped for a relaxing and tranquil time. That is not what we experienced. I think what we had not accounted for was the particular stresses of traveling with young children who needed supervision 24/7.

The proverbial straw that broke the camel's back came while food shopping. I was loading the cart with the children's favorites, including their preferred flavor of jelly. Howard, who better liked a different flavor, had a small fit. It was not like him to get upset over something so trivial, but I understood that it was just one thing among many that had worn him down. As we stood in the store, I could see his vacation expectations going down the drain.

A few nights later, we decided to take the children to a lovely steak house we had enjoyed when we had been there on our own. Unfortunately, the place was packed, and we had to wait two hours for a table. By the time we were seated, the children's heads were beginning to nod onto the table, and we were not so chipper either, having spent the day hiking the mountain trails.

Rather than taking the children's understandable fatigue in stride, Howard viewed their behavior as disrespectful. He kept telling them to sit up, that dinner was coming shortly, but those little heads kept drifting downward. By the time the food arrived, he was so upset and frustrated that when he dropped his fork, he refused to wait for a new one. He thrust his finger into the bowl of sour cream meant for the baked potatoes and ate it right from his finger.

Now it was my turn to get upset. In a loud voice, I berated him for being selfish, unkind, and childish. Looking back, I realize I was acting out of the same exhaustion he was—but the damage was done. Our nice evening out was ruined, and so was our vacation.

Anyone can lose patience with children, of course, and most parents do. Time passes, and what seemed earthshaking at that moment becomes a family story. (My daughter and I still talk about the "sour cream incident.") Suffice it to say that the middle years of *any* marriage can be difficult, and ours was no exception. The question becomes what the enduring, potentially damaging consequences are of the small resentments that build up during this period.

The underlying changes in roles and norms were chipping away at our marriage without our realizing it. Of course, we still loved each other. Was that not enough? If we were to just put one foot in front of the other and move along our path, would we make it safely through the forest? We continued to stumble on, too involved in day-to-day matters to notice that the witch was lurking and making her way closer to us.

I am now going to use an analogy that younger people might find foreign. Remember record players and how they worked? You would place the needle carefully onto the record, and music would pour forth. But sometimes the needle would get stuck and play the same bit over and over until you jumped up to move it ahead. When I realized our marriage had problems, the first image that came to mind was that stuck needle. We were stuck! We could not play the music properly unless we figured out how to fix things and move ahead. Heaven knows we did not want to be doomed to hear the same few notes over and over. Who can dance to that?

I certainly was not ready to throw away the record, and I knew Howard was not either. We were at a point where we had to make a choice: figure out a way to move the needle and allow the music to play on for the rest of our lives, or decide there was too much damage and toss the whole thing out. I think you know what we decided.

As we talked openly about our problems, we agreed that we were in the midst of a difficult period of life and would have to make some changes to get ourselves onto a better path. We would have to make time for introspection, self-exploration, and independent growth. If we were to grow as a couple, we would have to safeguard both our independence and our interdependence. Whether through exercise, reading, meditation, or hobbies, we both needed to regain our balance, strength, sense of self-worth, and inner happiness. Luckily for us, we could make these efforts within the close union we had formed throughout our years together. We may have come upon a few skips in the record, but we were not ready to toss out the player. We still had mutual respect and love, and with those things unshaken, we continued forward through the forest—old witch be damned.

CHAPTER 8

THE LATER YEARS (HANSEL AND GRETEL CHANGE TO SURVIVE)

"Life's just a perpetual piecing together of broken bits."
—Edith Wharton, *The Reef*

The fifth of the Greeks' six stages, pragma, is based on compromise, patience, and tolerance, all of which bring us to a deeper level of mutual understanding. This is how the strength of a marriage can become even greater. During this stage, the partners believe they will work together as a couple forever. This makes for many wonderful moments. To paraphrase psychologist Erich Fromm, who wrote *The Art of Loving*—we spend too much energy "falling in love" and need to learn more about how to "stand in love."

Giving this type of love freely to Howard was something I knew how to do from the time I was twenty, though I do not know why it came so easily to me. One of the biggest surprises in my life was that it did not come as easily to my husband. It was not until the later years of our marriage, when Howard was forced to face challenges in our relationship, that he was able to experience this fifth stage of love. He was forty-seven at that point. The good news is that once he made this leap, the twenty years that followed were by far our best. Perhaps you can now see why I am so committed to the benefits of following the six stages—and why I suggest working through them together as a couple. The next part of our story exemplifies the benefits of that process.

The last of the six stages, philautia, focuses on developing the capacity to love others. During this stage, we are aware of ourselves in relation to others beyond our marriage and, ideally, have learned to exist in the world in an unselfish manner.

Looking back, I see that as Howard and I grew older, philautia, like agape, did not develop smoothly or organically for him. Thus, the cracks between us widened even more. Both agape and pragma bring strength to a marriage, even when physical love declines due to age, illness, or another factor. Having lived through them all, I recognize that the six stages of love can provide a road map for moving together through a marriage as the journey unfolds.

As you have observed, the early stages of love—eros, philia, and ludus—came rather naturally to both Howard and me. We had no problems with intimacy. We were able to share, were loyal, and enjoyed a sense of trust.

In our late forties, after more than a quarter century of marriage, the minor cracks that had developed were actively growing wider and deeper. The needle on the record player was stuck, and we wondered if we would be able to move it. This was a very difficult time for us, both emotionally and financially. Howard's income decreased substantially, and he did not understand why. He would frequently complain that he felt like a hamster running endlessly on a wheel and never getting anywhere. He wanted to get off but did not know how, and his frustration and unhappiness affected us both.

Things slowly began crashing down, and we sensed we were imploding as a unit. In retrospect, I can see that much of this was caused by Howard's inability to develop through the last three stages of love, but at the time, it just seemed as though the constant pressure of suburban life was weighing us down. We felt pressured to keep up with the particular lifestyle that surrounded us, and it was simply too much to bear. *Where is our original life?* we wondered. *Where have "we" gone?*

While many people seem to love it, the conformity of suburban life was choking us. We had been raised in a city amid a diversity of people, ideas, and cultural experiences. By contrast, our life in the suburbs involved endless superstores and chain restaurants, occasionally relieved by a traveling musical or lesser museum. We longed for the individually owned small shops, restaurants, and groceries of our early lives, as well as the lively conversation within a diverse group of friends and acquaintances. We tired of trying to "keep up" and "fit in" where we did not belong, and it was taking a toll on our marriage.

As time went on, we became less capable of dealing with these challenges and felt stuck. After all, we were not kids anymore. We had professional careers and owned our home, and our children were doing well. The problem was us. Our life together was becoming smaller and smaller—claustrophobic. What could we do about this?

Our experience of home ownership had begun at the end of our middle years when our rental apartment was converted into a condominium, and we were informed that we would have to leave immediately. The condos were not going to permit dogs or children.

Not wanting to risk a repeat of this experience, we opted to purchase a small house using a VA loan. This meant we would not need to come up with a down payment we did not have (not that I understood much about that at the time). The place we found was a fixer-upper that we had no time to fix since we were both working six days a week.

A few short years after that, the universe smiled on us. An engineer-architect we knew wanted the property on which our house was located. We agreed to trade our fixer-upper (which he had the time and know-how to fix) for his larger, pristine house, provided we pay the difference in value.

This changed everything. Our happiness with our new home balanced out our misgivings about living in suburbia, so we stayed.

As I had spent my entire childhood in apartment buildings, having an acre of land (all that grass and a pool) was quite the experience! I no longer had to find a safe place for the children to play. I could walk out my back door and sit in a private yard to read rather than find a park bench or library for the purpose. Howard's reaction was similar. We could not believe our children would have this incredible opportunity—some transition for two kids from the block!

As we accustomed ourselves to our new surroundings, something unexpected happened. We had believed that a house was just a private structure made of wood, concrete, and paint, but we began to understand that it was more than that; it was *home*.

"We shape our buildings; thereafter they shape us," observed Winston Churchill in reference to rebuilding the House of Commons Chamber after its destruction during the German

Blitz. He understood that a building is more than a shelter; it is a place in which to build community, trust, and sanctuary. Howard and I came to believe that our home had great impact on our thoughts and feelings, and that the many windows that let light into our new space also enlightened *us*. That house became our center, our locus as individuals and as a close family. It has remained that ever since.

Frank Lloyd Wright, the architect known for his airy and livable homes, believed that the beauty of the exterior landscape could be brought inside. "More and more, so it seems to me, light is the beautifier of the building," he wrote. Our experience told us nothing could be truer.

Just as in fairy tales, the idea of admitting light into the darkness helped us transition from the dark experience of our first house to the light we found in our second. The architecture triggered an alchemical process whereby we moved from something ordinary into something greater: from a lower state to a higher one. Through the combination of form and space, a greater structure evolves, and the end result is that this new structure is greater than the sum of its parts.

The artist, not unlike the architect, manipulates natural light, using paint to create contrast and illuminate the darkness. Light and dark complement each other, and the painting transports the viewer to a higher place. This is the artist's alchemical process. Artists recognize that there can be no sense of light without the presence of darkness. This is as true in a long-term marriage as it is in art and architecture.

During our later years, we took a trip to Paris. We made a point of being there for the reopening day of the Musée de l'Orangerie in the Tuileries Garden, which had been closed for renovations for several years. Prominently displayed were eight paintings of water lilies from Claude Monet's *Nymphéas* series, bathed in the light between sunrise and sunset. A similar series also by Monet, *Haystacks,* captures the effect of light on a single object over time, seasons, and weather. Howard and I observed the world through the windows of our house in the same way, enjoying the changes in its beautiful light.

As I shared in chapter 5, Howard was happy doing most of the driving. For my part, I enjoyed "owning the kitchen." We had often spoken about the fact that my attitude toward driving paralleled his attitude toward cooking—which brings me to a brief kitchen story.

In 2004, we decided it was time to redo the kitchen. I knew my specific needs in that domain, and Howard enjoyed playing architect and planning the design. He pored over every detail as though it were one of his biology exams in college and employed his philosophy that the harder you work, the better the outcome.

We conferred and soon came to an agreement on the design, selecting appliances and cabinetry based on my needs and taste.

The owners of the kitchen shop we went to were quite impressed with Howard's efforts, which went so far as to include his bringing my favorite pan to the showroom to make sure it would fit into the sink they were recommending. During our final visit there, I noticed the showroom's model pantry with its copious shelves, compartments, and wine rack. I knew I was being a bit extravagant, but that pantry—it was as if it were made for me.

Howard took out his tape measure and checked a few things, examined the blueprints one more time, and said, "This is what she wants."

The owner of the company looked at Howard and replied, "You must love being in the kitchen with her!"

Howard and I just smiled at each other.

"You could not be more wrong," he told the man. "I do not enjoy cooking and Arlene is an excellent cook. I dislike even going into the kitchen—in fact, I would be quite happy never to go in there again."

The owner looked perplexed. "Then why are you so interested in the details of the design?"

"Simple," Howard said. "If Arlene gets exactly the kitchen she wants, I will get what I want: never to go into the kitchen again."

On that note, we left holding hands and enjoyed a lovely lunch. We were continuing to create a stronger whole—an entity that was more than the sum of its parts.

We believed we would live in that house forever and could not imagine any place more special. Although I cannot say we were gleefully happy every moment we lived there, we fully appreciated the happiness we shared. But, of course, life inevitably progresses and changes. First there were four of us in the house, then three, then two. Now there is just me.

Life's ups and downs came and went, but our home remained our safe space, where honesty, family, and pride flourished. We experienced celebrations, nightly dinner conversations, study sessions, teenager dilemmas, arguments, and moments of peaceful silence. The constant difficulties of ownership we had experienced in our fixer-upper gave way to the simple efficiencies of a modern house. It was smooth sailing now—or so we thought.

What I was not aware of—or did not want to be—was that a difficult stage in our marriage was slowly descending upon us. The cracks of our early and middle years had never been repaired, and all the magic in the world was not going to make them vanish. Add to that the fact that, although our house was delightful to live in, the large mortgage we had taken on it was beginning to exert its own form of pressure. Oblivious to all of it, Howard and I kept moving along our path through the woods without examining these matters. This is never a good thing.

CHAPTER 9

THE DARKNESS DESCENDS

*"Hope is being able to see that there is
light despite all the darkness."*

—Archbishop Desmond Tutu, South African
theologian and human rights activist

I t seemed to Howard and me that the larger challenges of
marriage tend to resolve themselves while you are dealing
with the smaller ones. Thus, we focused on work, driving
our children around, and all the other day-to-day matters that
keep working parents busy from morning till night. Meanwhile,
the forest through which we were walking was growing deeper
and darker.

Why did we—two smart, aware individuals—not notice what
was happening? Well, to offer yet another analogy, it was as if we
had been on a road trip and had at first encountered nothing but
green lights. Suddenly, we encountered a red light and dutifully
stopped—but the light would not change back to green! What
were we supposed to do? We had no idea. We should have seen
from afar that the green light had turned yellow—but, distracted

by the "scenery" of our daily lives, we had not noticed it. Now the red light had us at a standstill, and we had to examine the choices we had made.

We had chosen suburbia over city life, and the truth was, as much as we loved our house, we did not fit into our larger world. We had made critical errors regarding the pressures of home ownership and suddenly found ourselves traveling different paths instead of helping each other along the same one. Howard's role in our life together had changed too rapidly, and he could not work through it. The love stages of pragma and philautia that we should have been experiencing as a couple were eluding us.

Throughout our marriage, I believed I was committed to the role of the good wife. Looking back now, I see that the negative energy developing between Howard and me was affecting my ability to fulfill that role. My life was becoming about me, and Howard's life was becoming about him. We were losing our ability to work together to reinforce that third entity—*our marriage*—the thing that was stronger than either of us. I chose to move through our daily life experiences as best I could, ignoring the fact that Howard was not doing the same. Upon reflection, I wonder, was I responsible for this disjunction? Was it *my* responsibility to keep us on the right path, or was it both of ours?

I believed my purpose, first and foremost, was to create a stable family life and "stand by my man." So, even as our relationship grew more fractious and difficult by the day, I did not attempt to pull us together as a team. I had always worked full time, borne the brunt of raising our children, and done whatever I thought was expected of me. Now I found myself a continual object of blame for Howard's problems and frustrations. Thinking back on it, I recall a quote from author Bhavna Karnani Killa: "When you continue to be irritated by someone who refuses to change, you also refuse to change."

For many years, our relationship had been defined by intimacy, friendship, and trust. But the unaddressed stresses of those early and middle years were making it more difficult for us to move through the last three stages of love—those defined by selflessness, compassion, compromise, and the willingness to change. Those important qualities had simply not developed, and it really did not matter whose fault it was. It only mattered that our "third entity" was in trouble.

There came a point when we could no longer deny that while we remained afloat as individuals, our marriage was sinking. It was no longer greater than the sum of its parts—something we had always believed would remain.

At the time, we thought our journey together might be ending. Personally, I did not see any other possibility. I had come to the conclusion that Howard was unreachable and that I was walking through those dark woods alone.

The fateful night finally arrived. As we sat together in our beautiful living room, I announced, "I cannot live like this any longer. Our marriage is no longer a place where I can exist. I am done. You have to leave. I cannot be with you."

Clearly, Howard was shocked. When he seemed unable to accept what I was saying, I continued, "You have clearly come to believe that I am to blame for the mess we're in—for the stress and pressure and unhappiness you feel. While our life together has sometimes been hard, I never doubted that it was worth the struggle. But now . . . I feel I am watching what we built crumble and disintegrate."

I went on to remind him that when you begin dating at seventeen and share all of your "firsts," there is a certain strength that can carry you for many years. But that does not mean it is unbreakable or cannot be chipped away, piece by piece. I told him that I did not think I could revive what we had—that I was completely spent and, sadly, done.

Later that night—once again, in case he had not processed it the first time—I told my husband of twenty-seven years that he had to leave the home he had worked so hard to build because there was no love left in it.

What could he do? He packed a small bag and drove away that very night.

We agreed on one thing, at least: that the cloud was too dark, the darkness too bleak, and the emotional chasm too wide to continue on together. What we did not realize at the time was that, per the words of author Paulo Coelho, "not all storms come to disrupt your life; some come to clear your path."

Fortunately, we both knew we could manage independently, having built careers and a family. We had basically accomplished everything we had set out to do. Sadly, our dream had become a nightmare in the process.

Overwhelmed by exhaustion, I went to sleep. The next morning, I awoke early, as usual, and got ready for work. I was startled to see Howard's car outside and a note on the kitchen counter.

> I did leave, as you told me to, but after driving
> around for several hours, I realized I had nowhere
> to go. So, I am sleeping in the guest room, just
> until I figure something out.

For the next six days, we lived independently within our house. I would arrive home from work first and make sure to go to the bedroom before Howard returned from work. He would arrive later, after having eaten dinner, and would head straight to the guest room.

A week passed in this way, and on the following Saturday evening, Howard asked me to meet him in the family room. "We need to talk," he said.

As we settled ourselves, I looked at him and felt nothing.

"Arlene, . . . I'm going to leave. I will find a place to stay, at least temporarily. I know you're right; we're done. I can't live like this either, and I certainly don't want to."

A day later, as I stood quietly at our kitchen window, Howard left. I watched him get into his car, pull out of the driveway, and make a right turn toward the main road. When he reached the stop sign at the corner, I watched in disbelief as he turned the car around, drove back to the house, and let himself in.

"Howard, what—"

"Arlene, I accept the fact that our marriage is over, but . . . I think I need to talk this next part through with you. Do you think we could go somewhere and share a meal and talk?"

I sat silently for a few moments, then nodded. Feeling numb, I put on a sweater, grabbed my purse, and followed him out to the car.

We drove to a simple French bistro in a part of Miami we did not often visit. Once we were seated, we sat in silence for a few moments. This was Howard's idea, so I figured it was up to him to begin.

"I know I am not in a good place," he said, "and I also know you're not to blame for it. I can't make you love me or continue being my wife, but . . . I need your help, Arlene. Whether or not we continue our life together, I want to get better. And I need your help to do that. Will you help me?"

At that moment, I realized that agape, the Greeks' fourth stage of love, was developing in my husband right before my eyes. It is at this stage that a person must accept or reject the opportunity to make a change. Howard had previously been unable or unwilling to embrace change, but at this moment, he seemed to recognize that fact. And he seemed to want to make a new choice.

He lowered his head and whispered, "I want to be a better man."

It seemed that Howard was relying on all he knew about me: that I would always be his trustworthy partner and that I had his best interests at heart. And he was correct; even then I wanted only positive things for the man I had married.

A quote from the Indian philosopher Osho explains how I felt at that moment: "Awareness is the greatest alchemy there is. Just go on becoming more and more aware, and you will find your life changing for the better in every possible dimension. It will bring great fulfillment." I knew I had to help Howard. I knew he needed to become more fully aware of where our paths had diverged and of the path he had begun to follow on his own. Once he was more conscious, the choice to change would be up to him.

At that point, we both believed our marriage would end. But as two people with a long history and major investment in the life we had built, we committed to working toward a mutual understanding of why that was.

We were gearing up to employ our "Hansel and Gretel ingenuity"—our ability to work together to solve a problem and survive. We had no choice; the forest had grown too dark and dangerous for us to penetrate further.

Once I agreed to work with Howard toward a greater understanding, our next step was to discuss our options. We both had questions and concerns about how to proceed now that we had resigned ourselves to the fact that there was no longer an "us" or a "happily ever after."

Choices in fairy tales offer messages. A writer for the *Independent School Parent* site explained, "Even very young children are quick to work out that when a character in a fairy tale gets it wrong, there is usually a price to pay."[1] I understood that as long as honesty prevailed between us and that our choices about how to proceed were guided by a clear goal, there would be no punishment for either of us. We would own our mistakes and move on.

I was aware—and explained as best I could to Howard—that we had not made it through all six of the Greeks' stages of love. Clearly, the fissures in our marriage had steadily widened over time. Decisions regarding how to move on successfully as individuals had to be made. Howard had said he wanted to be a better man so that would have to be his primary goal. He would have to change if he did not want to drown in his own selfishness.

As for me, I had begun our marriage working full-time and had continued to do so, in spite of the fact that this was relatively unusual among our generation. At the same time, I had to fulfill all of the traditional "wifely" roles as well. Throughout all of it, we had never discussed the resentment that had taken root inside me as a result of this imbalance. Inevitably, my own resentment had bred resentment in Howard—a vicious cycle that had brought us to the edge of the terrible precipice we were facing.

Although I was overwhelmingly sad as I contemplated the death of my marriage, I could not see any other option. Howard could no longer be the center of my world around which I (and

---

[1] "Are Fairy Tales Still Relevant Today?" *Independent School Parent*, January 8, 2024. https://www.independentschoolparent.com/school/are-fairy-tales-still-relevant-today.

our children) revolved. At long last, I had to consider what was best for me rather than putting my husband first. In this process, I was progressing through philautia, the final stage of love; I was learning to love myself. Howard, on the other hand, was finally entering the fourth stage: agape.

I hope you do not think I considered myself perfect and a victim while Howard was the imperfect villain of our story. I had my own weaknesses and readily recognized them. I had closed myself off rather than deal with the cracks that had developed between us and focused primarily on the children and my career. There had been many times when I had seen the challenges we faced and did little to help surmount them. Sitting in that bistro with Howard, I knew I did not want him to suffer and feel like a failure for the rest of his life; we had both invested too much in our life together to allow things to end that way.

If we had any chance at all of moving forward successfully—either together or apart—I had to focus on one important fact. This was a man I had loved for a long, long time, based on qualities he had from the beginning and still possessed. A deep love like ours could not possibly just disappear without a trace of what had been. Howard had accomplished many significant things, and I needed to find a way to make him feel proud of those again. Yes, changes were warranted, but I had to convince him—and myself—that those changes were possible.

CHAPTER 10

THE DARKNESS AND
THE CAPTURE

"I now know that it is possible to experience post-traumatic growth. In the wake of the most crushing blows, people can find greater strength and deeper meaning."

—Sheryl Sandberg, *Option B: Facing Adversity,
Building Resilience, and Finding Joy*

E ven the happiest married couples can go through rough patches. What Howard and I did not realize when we hit what we believed was the wall that signified the end of our journey together was that we had been moving toward it for some time. We just had not been able to see it.

Hindsight, as they say, is 20/20. It is easy to see now that we had been willfully blinding ourselves to what was happening—or, at the very least, engaging in damaging behavior without concern for the inevitable repercussions. Several decades in, the damage had reached a point where it simply could not be ignored. We doubted—and did not dare hope—it could be reversed. Hansel and Gretel had gotten utterly lost along their way and then been captured by the witch.

Like Hansel, Howard was caged (in his case, within his own misery). Like Gretel, I despaired at being unable to find a way to save him. In the throes of our unhappiness, we lost sight of something extremely important: the fact that our marriage was itself an entity—and perhaps a stronger one than we had originally thought. Was it possible that this entity could withstand what we had done to it? If we could not save each other, could we save the marriage—and, in turn, could it save us?

At our lowest point as a couple, Howard was expressing a genuine desire to change. I believed he meant it, and I chose to help him. That transaction marked a new beginning for us, and it was the marriage itself that made it possible.

I have often referred to the rifts in our marriage as cracks that grew deeper over time. Whenever I use that simile, I picture a piece of fine china cracking under the pressure of constant use (or misuse). What is one to do with a beloved family heirloom that is no longer perfect and is getting worse by the day? Discarding it is always an option, but that feels like a last resort and not one to be taken lightly.

Applying glue might fix the problem temporarily, but the crack will probably return and grow even worse. So . . . what to do with the plate?

Reflecting on our marriage by way of this analogy, I remembered the Japanese technique known as *kintsugi*. If you were wondering about the image on the front cover of this book, it is an illustration of exactly this. In Japan, when a dish or piece of pottery is broken, kintsugi is a way to make it useful again while honoring its history.

The word *kintsugi* (sometimes called *kintsukuroi)* means *mending with gold* or *golden joinery.* The art form dates back to the fifteenth century and is a painstaking process that can take months or even years. Pieces of the shattered object are gathered, then gently cleaned and carefully reassembled using multiple coats of resin mixed with gold. The effect is as if flowing metal has fused the pieces back together, becoming an integral part of the object itself. No attempt is made to hide where the breaks once were; in fact, they are accentuated. Rather than discarding the broken item, one is making it even more beautiful than it was before, more honest about its own history, and it remains as useful as ever. It embraces imperfection in plain sight.

So, how does kintsugi relate to marriage? When we are un-happy in a marriage, we have the option to end it. If, however, we choose not to discard it but to honor it by mending it, we are engaging in a form of kintsugi: applying a beautiful and visible "fix" that acknowledges the experience as a whole. While we may not be able to eliminate or even hide the cracks and damage we have sustained, we can work to repair our marriage—our third entity—in a way that honors its history and makes it even stronger, more honest, and more beautiful. Perhaps we can then view it as a golden journey.

In those moments when I was deciding whether to try to move forward with Howard or separate from him, I came to the conclusion—or, at least, the hope—that we might be capable of incorporating our wounds into our marriage rather than giving up and discarding the beautiful, useful "object" we had designed and made together and put into use for all those years.

Not to belabor the analogy, but that piece of kintsugi-repaired pottery has served me as such a useful symbol—at once fragile and strong, breakable and resilient, precious and utilitarian. In those dark days, I hoped that by attempting to mend our marriage with kintsugi in mind, Howard and I just might be making it stronger than ever while honoring the scars it had sustained in its service to us. And those visible points of reattachment would remind us of the mistakes we had made and their cost.

You could say that the art of kintsugi, when applied to a relationship, is another form of alchemy. The alchemist brings elements together, while the kintsugi artist brings broken pieces together. As Howard and I worked things out, we, too, were creating our version of gold.

There is another Japanese concept I find pertinent to marriage and its alchemy, something known as *wabi-sabi*. It is a philosophy based on the appreciation and acceptance of imperfection in life and the acknowledgment that the world is fundamentally changeable and challenging. Developing an appreciation for wabi-sabi—a kind of random "messiness"—means letting go of perfection and ideal forms of beauty and, instead, appreciating life's flaws and imperfections. Those who embrace wabi-sabi understand that seeing the beauty in imperfection can pave the way for personal growth. When Howard and I learned to discuss our flaws openly, it was a major step forward for us.

I think you can see how both kintsugi and wabi-sabi served us as more than just analogies. The philosophy behind them provided us with actual tools for approaching the daunting task of repairing and, ultimately, strengthening our union. In the end, two of the most important things we discovered were that we did not have to regret the past and that we could still write the future.

CHAPTER 11

THE CONVERSATIONS BEGIN

"Yesterday I was clever, so I wanted to change the world. Today I am wise, so I am changing myself."

—Rumi, thirteenth-century Persian poet

While I understood the benefit of talking things out with Howard, I knew it would be a long and complex process—one in which we would both have to set aside what we thought we knew and open ourselves to what was really happening. It would take a lot of time, and we would have to let the conversation unfold slowly and within an atmosphere of affection and mutual support. Howard and I were on a precipice, and I feared we did not have the luxury of time for that—so I decided we would have to proceed in another way.

I wanted to give Howard the help he had asked for in understanding how things had become so broken, even though we both knew it was unlikely to "fix" our marriage. I saw it as an opportunity to help him move from a place of self-centeredness to a higher level along the six stages of love: that of collaboration and caring for others. And, as Cinderella sings in the musical *Into the Woods,* "Opportunity is not a lengthy visitor."

All of the significant relationships in Howard's life were slipping away as his sadness overwhelmed him, and I understood the urgency of arresting this process. Instead of entering into a free-form dialogue, I suggested we skip right to some direct and difficult topics. To ease our way into them, I explained my feelings deliberately and carefully.

"Howard," I began, "I will love you my entire life. I always have, and I always will. But I have come to understand the differences between loving someone, adoring him, and being *in love* with him. I will always have that first piece and am genuinely grateful that I have also experienced the second. Sadly, I no longer have the last one—the *in-love* part of our relationship. It was the basis of our marriage, and now it is gone. That said, because of our long history and our children, I want to help you."

Howard just nodded, so I continued. "I will ask for nothing in return," I said. "You can keep all the money you earned with your hard work, and I'll continue to work to support myself. I promise to help you through this painful transition, but I have a few non-negotiable conditions."

Again, Howard uttered not a word of protest.

"Each morning, we will sit together and have a cup of coffee on a bench in the park."

Benches had played a significant role in our journey, and I knew this was not lost on Howard.

"I will do my best to make you see the negative behaviors you have been exhibiting and the impact they have had on those closest to you. I will focus on your acts of selfishness, and you will listen to me without protest. Only when I am finished telling

you all of this, and I genuinely believe you have heard me, can we begin our conversation."

Perhaps this sounds selfish on my part—seizing an opportunity to air my grievances without protest—but I knew this was our only path to a productive dialogue. If this process was going to work, I would have to lead the way.

We were both quiet for a moment, and then Howard sighed, lifted his head, and said, "I guess our marriage has drifted away from both of us—which is ironic to me since we've always worked so hard at everything. I know that I trust you and you trust me, but I understand that isn't enough. We've become separate, and I guess that in order to come back together, I'll need to fix myself."

I could not resist a small smile. It was as if Howard were seeing through new eyes.

"Arlene," he continued, finally meeting my gaze, "I get that you want to explore the road that got us here. Okay. I'm willing to try it your way. Maybe you're right, and it's the only way for us to find happiness for ourselves, even if we remain separate."

He did not mention my insistence on the bench, but I knew he understood its purpose. I have always maintained that sitting outside in nature can help people slow down, connect, and just *be*. By their very design, park benches are perfect for two people who want to be close and relate to each other. Think about the iconic bench in the film *Forrest Gump*. When another person joins Forrest on it, he is moved to share his history, philosophy, and yearning for connection.

When Howard and I first met, way back in college, I remember thinking, *He is a nice boy, well-meaning and focused; he is like me.* All these years later, I knew that nice boy was still in there somewhere. I believed I could find a way to alter his perspective and help him regain his genuine concern for others. The only tools I had were my words, so they would have to be enough.

Before I move on to the next part of our story, I want to share a little flashback I had as I laid out my plan for Howard. We were eighteen-year-old college students and had been dating for a little while. To earn some extra money, Howard took a holiday job sorting mail at the post office in Downtown Brooklyn over the December-to-January holiday break. (Remember, there were no computers back then, no UPS delivery, and no overnight Amazon. The post office became overwhelmed during the Christmas holidays and very much needed short-term help.)

A few weeks prior to this time, on a Saturday study break, we had taken a stroll to window-shop, and I had noticed a beautiful tawny-brown suede coat. "Oh!" I exclaimed. "How perfect!" That was before I noticed its eighty-dollar price tag. In 1966, there was no way we or any of our friends would have had that kind of money for such an extravagance. (It could not even have been worn in the rain!)

You have probably guessed this, but Howard scraped together nearly all of his earnings from his twelve-hour-a-day postal job and bought me that coat. To him, it was worth every penny just to see the smile on my face and feel the warmth in my heart when he delivered it.

I will say it again: I believed that nice boy was still inside my husband.

I said a silent prayer that I would be able to find the right words to reach Howard and that he would hear them in the right spirit. Ultimately, I hoped he would translate those words into a way to regain the trust and love of his family—particularly his children—as well as that of his friends and colleagues. Yet again, I am moved to contradict what I noted at the beginning of this book: that neither Howard nor I was a hero in our story. I eventually came to believe that the courage it takes to change after twenty years of marriage can be considered a heroic act.

Although he understood he might get hurt, Howard trusted my plan and chose to face all I had to tell him. He had no idea whether he would be able to swim in the ocean of change I was hurling him into, but he promised he would try. Our conversations would last only a few months, but they would be the catalyst for a rebirth of our marriage—nothing less.

What I hope to impart here, by sharing our conversations as well as my philosophy of marriage in general, is that marriage evolves through numerous stages as it becomes an entity of its own. And at a moment of truth such as the one Howard and I faced, that entity can provide a reason to accept change. Our marriage, even in a time of crisis, could provide a safe space in which we could explore our strengths and weaknesses, learn to encourage each other, and respond to each other's needs.

As the fifth stage of love, pragma, emerged in Howard, he gained patience for the process we needed to go through. It became clear to me that this would be an opportunity for us to explore and grow, both as individuals and as a couple.

"Please keep in mind," I told him, "that I believe there are two types of selfishness. The first is the good type, which involves setting boundaries and making choices to improve one's own life and, ultimately, have a positive impact on others. The second kind of selfishness is not as good. It means doing things for oneself at the expense of others. You have experienced both. In the conversations we're going to have, I intend to tell you honestly how I believe your behavior over the past few years has morphed from the first type of selfishness into the second. Once I've shared my observations with you, you'll have some choices to make about your future."

The Conversations

> "Was it you or I who stumbled first? It does not matter. The one of us who finds the strength to get up first, must help the other."
>
> —Vera Nazarian, author

As I pondered where our first conversation should begin, I thought about the mistakes Howard had made in his business, which was, at that point, falling apart. Perhaps that would be the least painful place to start. I knew in my heart it was the underlying challenges of marital life that had seeped through and created his business problems, but I had to start somewhere.

We drove together and settled on our bench without saying more than a few words. As we opened the lids on our coffees, I could not help reflecting on the significance of the bench itself. I had made the right choice in bringing us here, where we were surrounded by fresh air and nature. "The goal of life is living in agreement with nature. Well-being is attained little by little, and nevertheless is no little thing itself," noted the Greek philosopher Zeno of Citium, and I agree 100 percent.

In the conversations we were about to begin, I would be revisiting places and actions from our past. It was important that we be in a place where we could recall them clearly and understand that each moment of our history was part of a journey—possibly to something better and more beautiful. (As in the process of kintsugi I described earlier, we would be honoring even the damage we had sustained by making it an invaluable part of the whole.) On that bench, I hoped we could connect our inner world with the limitless outer one.

I began by addressing Howard's life as a whole. "I realize that your choices over the years were not part of some Machiavellian plan," I noted. "You did not wake up one morning and say, 'How can I sabotage my life and my marriage?' You made many choices, one by one, over a long period of time, and they had consequences. Had you been able to consider alternative choices, consult others as equals, and listen carefully to their opinions, you might have acted differently."

He held my gaze and sipped from his cup.

"Let's talk about your work, for starters. I think that if you had respected and consulted the people who worked with you in your office, they might have made suggestions that would have benefited the business. You worked hard and achieved much, but your behavior toward others left you alone at the top, in peril of falling off a cliff and without the benefit of others' wisdom. To your credit, most of them are still with you and still willing to help."

"I know this," he said simply and looked down at his shoes. "Arlene, . . . I have to tell you honestly that I am terrified about the pain that's going to come from these conversations. But I think maybe my fear is worse than the conversations will be! I've decided . . . I just have to trust you and listen to what you have to say."

By offering me this trust and his willingness to continue, Howard was embodying Paulo Coelho's notion that "there is only one thing that makes a dream impossible to achieve: the fear of failure."

I chose not to linger too long that first day, knowing that Howard was committed to the process and we could take our time. The next several conversations we had focused on his actions and choices in both his work and home life, and the impact they had on those around him. These examples were a way of illustrating the stages of love he had not fully achieved: agape, pragma, and philautia. His inability to move through these stages had led him to make decisions based primarily on what was best for him. He had developed a habit of excluding others, as evidenced by his actions.

Returning to his troubles in the workplace, I reminded him of a tragic time some ten years earlier when his office manager's son had committed suicide. "That boy was only seventeen, and Mary was most naturally devastated," I said. "And while you did give her the time off she felt she needed, you made no effort to reach out to her directly and express sympathy."

Howard lowered his head in recognition.

"This was something everyone in the office made note of. Rather than using this as a time to unify your staff and show them by example how empathy can strengthen a community, you exhibited tunnel vision. You simply did your job and waited for Mary to return. Once she did, you left her to her own devices. This is an example of how you have placed your own needs ahead of the needs—sometimes profound—of those in your circle.

"What's worse," I continued, "is that, in the few weeks Mary was away, you ordered all new and unfamiliar computer equipment. How was she supposed to transition to a completely new system she was not a part of choosing, was not trained on, and did not have any idea how to use, so soon after losing a child?

"Miraculously, Mary did manage to rise to the occasion. Your way of rewarding her was to pile on more responsibilities. And because you did not take proper care of her when she needed it, her weak emotional state continued to impact everything she did going forward.

"I'm sure you know that this is just one example of a pattern of behavior on your part. You frequently offloaded responsibility onto another without considering whether that person was physically or emotionally capable of accomplishing it. By focusing exclusively on what you needed or wanted, you let everything go awry. Your office fell into shambles, and while you were eager to blame everyone but yourself, the reality is that the problems grew out of your own selfishness—that second type. So, where has this left you? Trying to figure out the problems with the computer system on your own while financial problems are impacting our entire life."

At this point, Howard lost control. "What you don't understand, Arlene, is that I was drowning!" he shouted. "Without Mary, I had nowhere to turn, and it made me angry; it almost paralyzed me. I am trying to see it differently now—honestly— but at the time, I believed you were the problem, the office was the problem, and I was the victim. Alone. Stuck."

Feeling his pain in reliving those times, I understood his anger. "Howard," I said softly, "I had no idea what you were going through. But I felt your anger, and it made me angry in return.

Looking back, I can see that we were falling down that rabbit hole and picking up momentum as we fell."

That conversation went on for quite a while, and at the end of it, we were as empty as our coffee cups.

The next day, I began our talk with some genuine words of encouragement.

"Howard, . . . I know you will ultimately turn things around at work. I know without a doubt that you will fix things because I know who you are deep down."

"I was so angry," he said. "So very angry, but I see now that it was mainly at myself for feeling like a failure. I thought I was drowning and desperately wanted someone to throw me a life preserver. Why wouldn't you or anyone else help me? I can see now, though . . . why would anyone want to? I'd been so selfish for so long."

Clearly, Howard had become overwhelmingly disappointed in himself to the point where he was inconsolable. This disappointment had manifested itself as hostility toward others and a tendency to place blame anywhere but where it belonged.

As he had promised, Howard tried hard to listen to what I was saying, and slowly, he processed it. More conversations took place, some of which left him unable even to swallow his coffee. And it was not just Howard who was overwhelmed with emotion. I, too, became so choked up at times that I could not speak. It was all part of a process that, admittedly, was hardest on Howard, but it was hard on me as well.

Naturally, our conversations soon turned to the subject of family interactions.

"You were a great provider," I began one morning. "You gave the children every opportunity to succeed and flourish. Consequently, they are launching themselves into their own lives and doing very well. But . . . while they did live under your roof, you always made sure your needs were met first. Theirs—and mine—were met as well, but those were secondary."

"I . . . believe you, Arlene, but . . . what was it that I did wrong?"

"It was not what you did, Howard. It's what you did not do. You did not listen to them or learn from any situation we found ourselves in. The children simply obeyed you. Your decisions were final, without regard for what the rest of us might need or want. We had meals based on your schedule, outings, everything. You were the decision-maker. In fairness, I was responsible for some of this as well, and it was partly due to the expectations of the era in which we grew up. We were both raised to see the male as the dominant member of the household. But your complete embrace of this role—your arrogance—led us down a path of little communication and lots of discontent. Everyone wants to be seen and heard, and often in our house, the children and I felt neither."

For the first time in our series of talks, Howard challenged me: "I understand this is how you feel, Arlene, but how do I know the children really feel this way? Maybe you are just projecting."

I thought about what he said and realized he had a point. The last thing I wanted to do was put words in the mouths of my very adult children, who were perfectly capable of speaking for themselves.

"Good point, Howard; I am glad you raised it. Here's my cell phone. Call Mara, and ask her yourself. Frame it any way you'd like. Tell her what I've said, and ask her what she has to say. I promise you, it will be the first she's heard that we are even having these conversations."

After a moment of thought, Howard took me up on my suggestion. He accepted my phone and pressed a few buttons, and soon Mara answered from her college dorm room.

"Mom?"

"No, honey, it's Dad."

Howard went on to explain that he and I were having an important conversation, and he needed her input. How would she characterize his behavior during the years she was growing up? Would she say he had been arrogant or difficult?

Clearly, Mara was nervous. "I . . . I don't really feel comfortable answering that, Dad," she said. "I . . . don't want to be disrespectful."

"Mara, I appreciate that—and I promise, I won't be mad at you or hurt, no matter what you say—but I need you to tell me honestly how you feel about this. What was I like as a father?"

Still uncertain about the whole conversation, Mara asked her father to repeat his promise that he would stay calm no matter what she said.

"I promise," he reiterated.

"Dad, you were a great father—the best. You gave us everything. But you behaved like an asshole much of the time. No matter how hard we tried to talk to you honestly about what was going on with us, you never heard us. You never listened."

When Howard was silent, Mara continued, "Dad, you wanted to know. You promised not to get mad. And, Dad, I love you. No matter what."

After a brief thank-you, Howard ended the call and handed me back the phone. "Arlene, we have to go," he said. "I just cannot talk anymore."

Mara's words had hit him hard because he knew they were the truth. I believe that this was the moment he truly committed to changing. This was the moment he began to understand the idea behind the words of author Erin Morgenstern, "There is no fixing. There is only moving forward in the brokenness."

CHAPTER 12

FROM CONVERSATION TO CHANGE

"God gave Adam a secret—and that secret was not how to begin, but how to begin again."

—Elie Wiesel, Holocaust survivor and Nobel laureate

There was nothing passive about the conversations Howard and I were having. They were part of a slow process that involved no anger, only a painful journey two people continually chose to endure. I was careful not to bring up any specific arguments from the past. I discussed only those behaviors that had harmed Howard's relationships with me, our children, and his colleagues—anything I felt he had to be aware of and change in order to move forward.

It was with great sadness that I detailed for my husband how he had compromised his most important relationships and created a situation in which he had no support system during a time of great need. (Well, he had me, at least for the duration of this process—but that, we had agreed, was a finite period of time.)

The more we talked, the more our conversations resonated with Howard. Gradually, he began to internalize what he was learning and think about how this knowledge might govern his choices in the future. The first step was recognizing that he stood alone and that unless he became a better man, he would continue to be alone.

Howard trusted me, and over the days that followed, he became more and more certain that he wanted to change. "I want to be a better man," he told me more than once, and I knew it was true.

The psychotherapist David Richo, best known for his book *How to Be an Adult,* wrote, "What we are not changing, we are choosing." When I quoted this to Howard, I could see that it had real meaning for him. Just a few weeks earlier, it would have gone right over his head.

Maybe you are wondering why I insisted we undertake these conversations on our own rather than bringing a therapist into the equation. I assure you that it is not because I am against therapy, which can be a godsend for many couples, whether they end up staying together or separating. How to navigate a marital crisis is an important decision each couple must make for itself. All I can do here is tell you how I chose to handle *our* crisis and that my decision was based on my deepest instincts about our long and (for the most part) satisfying relationship.

Talking had always been something Howard and I had done well and honestly—until it was not. I hoped and believed that, for all we had lost track of, we could still talk ourselves back onto a path that led us where we needed to go. In taking that leap of faith, I was governed by the words of poet Maya Angelou, who said, "Have enough courage to trust love one more time and always one more time."

So we talked. And gradually, Howard began to see that the people in his life had not changed; they had simply chosen to move away from him. And by "people," I mean those with whom he had important long-term relationships. Howard had been married to me for twenty-seven years, had been a father for twenty, and had known some of his office mates for decades. But that had not stopped any of them—any of us—from backing away from a man whose choices and actions had become more and more selfish.

"What can I do?" Howard asked me plaintively, as if I might have a simple answer.

What could he do?

I was there to help him, but I struggled with what to advise. I reminded him that he had already taken an important first step by committing to becoming a better man. Now he would have to make those around him believe in this commitment through actions. He had talked the talk, but now he had to walk the walk, and the road would not necessarily be a smooth one. He was going to have to slow down, remain mindful, and review each choice and action from multiple perspectives. He would have to consider his life from the viewpoints of those important to him.

Howard's behavior over the preceding years had tarnished the trust of his colleagues and loved ones—and trust is the basis for strong and productive relationships. It is what carries us through our most difficult times, and Howard very much needed trusting allies around him at that point. To regain these, he would have to ask himself, *Is what I am about to do going to bring people closer to me or push them further away?*

As we talked these things through, I was encouraged to see that philautia, the crucial sixth stage of love, was evolving within Howard. He was translating his capacity to love himself into a genuine ability to love others simply by becoming more aware of who he was in relation to me, our family, and his colleagues. We had all loved him once, and if he were to regain some measure of that love, it would come only with trust.

Over the next several months, Howard began a process of talking to each key person in his life. He asked them what they needed from him and tried hard to listen to their answers. One tough conversation at a time, he began to understand his loved ones and what was important to each of them.

Not surprisingly, he started this process with me, knowing I already understood what he was trying to accomplish and had faith that he could succeed.

"I need to explain myself to you, our children, and my colleagues," he declared. "And I need to begin with you. We had no prearranged life plan when we started out, but we were always in step. Somewhere along the way, we went wrong—or I went wrong—to such a degree that you are done with me and with this marriage. The thing is, I don't have any desire to move on without you. I want us to work through it all, step by step if necessary, and figure out what went wrong."

Naturally, this moved me. "You and I may have had no life plan," I said, "but we did have goals. It's just that sometimes, in reaching for those goals, we ended up moving in different directions. The point now is to figure out whether there's any hope that we can move back toward each other or at least understand what pulled us apart so we can move on in our own directions."

Even as our own talks continued, Howard decided that he would initiate private conversations with our children as well. To each of them in turn, he explained, "I am coming to you now as a father who has made mistakes but who now wants to grow—and grow with you. You are at an age where it is natural to keep growing and learning. For my sake, and for the sake of our family, I want to join you in that. As old as I am, I don't think it's too late for me."

Rather than getting bogged down in past actions, Howard worked hard to keep these dialogues in the present. He asked our children about their current lives, hopes, dreams, and challenges, and rather than judging their responses, he asked how he could bring value to their lives. He understood that his children were now adults and did not need him in the ways they had when they were young. But he hoped to establish what they did need out of a relationship with him and was determined to fulfill it.

His next task was to repair his relationships with his office colleagues. Unlike a regular dental office, an orthodontic office tends to enjoy a more lighthearted atmosphere. Many of the patients are young, and those who are adults are excited to improve their health and appearance with long-awaited dental work. For many years, laughter was always in the air in Howard's office, but this changed as his temperament grew darker. What had been sunny grew cloudy, and people who had been with him for decades sorely needed his attention and reassurance.

He chose to begin his process of reclamation with stories from their shared past. "I remember when our office was filled with fun," he told a few of them, assembled around the lunch table at his invitation. "We used to have lunches together like this all the time. Remember when Sheri offered to get Chinese takeout, and I told her to bring back a variety of dishes, including one chicken, one shrimp, and one beef?"

Those who remembered the incident were already smiling.

"She did *that* all right," he continued. "She came back with chicken lo mein, shrimp lo mein, and beef lo mein! We just laughed until we were gasping. And remember all the crazy holiday photos we worked so hard to set up? They were so wacky that our patients waited all year for them."

While everyone around the table was nodding and chuckling at the memory, Howard continued on a more serious note. "I know my actions over the last couple of years have eroded all that goodwill and dampened everybody's spirits," he said. "I know that I haven't really been here for all of you in the way I should have, leading and inspiring the team, like in the old days. Thank goodness Arlene has helped me see that I have some changes to make and a lot to make up for. I am here today to tell you I am committed to bringing back the passion, the joy, and the sense of teamwork we shared when this place was at its best. Not only that, but also, I want you all to know that *I* know I could not have succeeded all these years without you and your hard work, ideas, and input. I can't succeed in this personal process without you either. I am working hard to make a lot of changes in my life, and some of them are going to happen right here—with your help."

After sharing a few more funny memories in which he was the butt of the joke—just to make his genuine humility clear—Howard moved on to what was ahead for them as a team. He told me later that he could feel his employees reopening their hearts to him, never more so than when he asked them  for their help. While he may not have won back their full trust in this initial conversation, he had certainly made a good start.

In just a couple of months, Howard had made a lot of progress with both his children and his colleagues, and it was clear to me that he was committed to continuing the process in both areas of his life. I knew he felt good about this, but I also knew that above and beyond any of it, he wanted one thing: me.

Changes in Perspective

> "In all affairs it's a healthy thing now and then to hang a question mark on all of the things you have long taken for granted."
>
> —Bertrand Russell, philosopher

During his months of hearing, listening, and processing my words and those of others, Howard slowly began to grasp the importance of perspective. By honestly assessing the perspectives of others, he was learning to make better decisions. He saw that he had been out of step with those around him—that his interactions had been disjointed and that only he could shift them into place. We likened it to the act of tuning a radio dial until you find the point of clearest reception. Only after properly "tuning in" to other people could he see the bigger picture of his communal experiences.

"Howard, how do you want to live the next part of your life?" I asked him one day. I told him not to answer me directly but to think about it and then to consider what he would have to do to make that life possible.

As retired professor of oral literature Kay Stone writes in reference to the heroes in fairy tales, "Heroes succeed because they act, not because they are. They are judged . . . by their ability to overcome obstacles, even if these obstacles are defects in their own character." Like the best of these characters, Howard was now experiencing the fourth stage of love, agape. He was developing the ability to choose to change and internalize a new way of being within his everyday life.

Once Howard had broadened his perspective, he could change his actions toward others. Again, he started this work with me, and that meant diving into a strong, difficult current. Slowly but surely, he changed. Acts of kindness became his default setting again. He regained his ability to be present for those he cared about and sensitive to their needs, and he methodically mended his relationships with those who had become distant or completely estranged. Ultimately, Howard created an atmosphere of trust within which we could all dwell safely.

Perhaps this sounds downright miraculous, but I assure you it is true. Howard was successfully transitioning to a life reflecting the Japanese concept of *ikigai*, which requires genuine motivation and a sense of purpose. To achieve ikigai, a person must pursue his passions and use his talents for the betterment of the world around him. And that is what Howard did. He soon began to see that everything around him had the potential to become better—his entire life's journey could proceed on a better course. He grew determined that his story would be one of transformation rather than one of repeating old behaviors in an endless cycle. He would let go of past guilt, resentment, and bitterness in favor of hope and the joy of true connection. Once again, alchemy would play its part, turning debased and undervalued relationships and experiences into golden ones.

A transition of this magnitude can occur gradually, as it did for Howard, or in one overwhelming second, as it did for me when our daughter was giving birth to her daughter. Mara and her husband, Tracey, had invited me to be in the delivery room right up until the actual delivery took place; that moment would be theirs alone. I was delighted to be part of the overall experience and quite content with their parameters, which made perfect sense to me.

As the baby was about to enter the world, I started to leave the room.

"Please stay," said my son-in-law, grasping my hand.

Shocked, I protested. "Tracey, this is your moment!"

He held fast to my hand and looked straight into my eyes. "You belong here," he said firmly.

I looked down at my daughter, and she nodded her assent—so I stood quietly by as the baby arrived and Tracey cut the umbilical cord. His decision in those precious moments—to include me in the experience—was made out of kindness, but he had no idea of the impact it would have on me.

My presence in that delivery room allowed me to witness a true love transition in which I was playing a part. I had always known that my daughter loved me more than any other human being (love for a spouse being very different). She and I were bonded; we were one. But when that baby was placed into her arms, her eyes, her face, her body, her whole being transferred all the love that had existed between us directly to her new daughter. I knew right then that although she and I would always be bonded, her new greatest love was for that child. The feeling that inspired in me was sheer, unadulterated joy that a circle of life had been completed.

A year later, I was once again privileged to be in the delivery room with Mara and Tracey, and once again, I witnessed the dawning of unmatched love between my daughter and her newborn girl. It occurred to me that the deepest forms of love grow and change as needed in order for new bonds to be created.

Reflecting on that, I understood how Howard might now be able to create new bonds that were even stronger than the old ones. While my daughter's transition had been by nature, his would be by choice or "nurture." In other words, he would have to nurture it through communication, compromise, and commitment—elements of the last three stages of love: agape, pragma, and philautia.

Even as Howard was working to change his perspective, I was developing my own way of viewing my life. For one thing, I began to rethink the concept of kintsugi. I thought about the cracked plate repaired noticeably with gold. Would a visible crack in my marriage always inspire a shiver of sadness over what had been broken? Or might it remind me, as Ernest Hemingway put it in *A Farewell to Arms,* that we can be "strong at the broken places"?

An understanding of alchemy (as well as kintsugi) helped me see that a cracked and repaired object might be even more beautiful—and more durable—than the original. If Howard and I could view our failures, mistakes, and imperfections as essential aspects of our history, might we emerge with an even stronger and more precious relationship than we had before? Howard was beginning to understand the difference between *need* and *want* in a marriage—that while we might need each other, wanting each other was different. He said, "I believe you and I have needed each other since the beginning. What I never really understood was how much I wanted you. And then, when our children came along, I wanted and needed them too, and I did not understand that either. And I had no clue what any of you needed or wanted from me."

He went on to say I brought balance to his life, and he knew now that being worthy of our marriage meant valuing my needs above his own. That declaration was a turning point for me and gave me more hope than I had felt since things had first begun to fall apart. It was wonderful to hear that Howard still needed and wanted me, but feeling him work toward a means to that end was the best aspect of a process that was taking a lot out of both of us.

In coming to an understanding of what he had taken for granted and squandered, Howard now wanted it more than ever. We were slowly evolving into something greater than the sum of us. As a young Henry David Thoreau wrote in his journal, "There is no remedy for love but to love more."

In the months that followed, Howard told me that, as a scientist as well as a husband, he believed that I was his fulcrum but also much more. I was his light, his fire. As he saw it, bringing me back to him would involve putting together exactly the right combination of elements.

Howard explained it in terms based on ancient alchemy and latter-day chemistry: "You are the catalyst," he declared, "the fire transforming us. Together, we are gold." He could now see as clearly as I did that our marriage was indeed a third entity, stronger than either of us individually.

Having witnessed his transformation, I am more confident than ever that although each person in a marriage is independent, the two are also *interdependent*. We yearn for the touch and warmth of our partners, their wisdom, humor, kindness, and closeness. In that way, we are dependent. But the strength we gain from that connection makes us both independent and interdependent—stronger as individuals because of the third entity we have formed. I have to wonder, can anyone who does not understand the alchemy of marriage understand love? All I know is that I am filled with gratitude that I understand and appreciate that alchemy, and that Howard came to understand it as well.

I may have helped him become a better man (I certainly tried), but in the process, I grew and evolved as well. The result was pure gold.

Howard's focus then turned to his children. In a process similar to the one he went through with me, he approached each one individually, working to understand their needs and wants and how he had to change to fulfill them.

Of course, they both needed and wanted him; he was their father. Likewise, he came to see how much he wanted them. The relationships were what mattered, not anyone's role or status in the family, and Howard dedicated himself to approaching them in that spirit.

Based on his conversations with each child, he determined what actions he needed to take. He risked his hearing to attend a heavy-metal rock concert and once endured a weeklong ice-fishing trip in Minnesota. Whatever the activity, his goal was to bond with his children and spend time sharing the passions of each of them. For the first time, he was prioritizing what was important and meaningful to them—and they felt it.

Howard told me that he had begun his conversations with both of them by quoting the author Cole Todd, who said, "Everyone should have the experience of getting lost in life at least once. Part of growing up is learning how to tolerate uncertainty, and when the time is right, to find or create a new path for yourself." Howard went on to explain that he knew it was he who needed to grow up, not them. Both children shared that Howard was honestly providing them with a path back to him. Mara told me, "When Dad was willing to participate in our lives, doing what we enjoyed, giving us time and really having fun with us, we realized how much he needed us and wanted us. And he didn't give up halfway through, either. He kept at it until we trusted the 'new him' completely."

Howard's attempts to repair things with his colleagues did not involve any trips to rock concerts or ice-fishing holes, but he did share a version of the Cole Todd quote with them. Mainly, he focused on the power dynamics in the office and how he hoped to change them. He listened as they told him how he might have behaved differently, and then he told them honestly how he thought they might have better handled certain challenges. Working together, Howard and his team created a blueprint for the future that they all believed would make their office life better and more productive. An unexpected benefit of the process was that some creative and valuable new ideas emerged. When Howard's employees were encouraged to combine their ideas with his, exciting prospects for growth emerged.

Once Howard had committed to altering his perspective, he was able to alter his behavior—prompting me once again to ponder the definition of *hero*. Howard may not have seemed like one of those fairy tale princes or dragon slayers, but his determination to change his life and the actions he undertook to do so certainly describe a hero's journey—at least from my perspective. After all, a fairy tale is just someone's story, and within everyone's unique story is the possibility of his or her becoming a hero. As Hans Christian Andersen pointed out, "Life itself is the most wonderful fairy tale." And as Howard himself noted, "The harder you work, the luckier you get!"

When I reflect upon the use of the word *chemistry* as it applies to two people in a relationship, I recognize that over time, it becomes emotional as well as physical. I have learned that there is no advance warning for the aha moments in life. They just hit you. They stop you and overwhelm you. At the beginning of this book, I posited that marriage has a life of its own. I came to believe this during the tumultuous time that followed twenty-seven years of marriage.

Toward the end of the three months we spent in conversation about our situation, I had one of those aha moments. I was walking across the house, and I heard a voice in my head that demanded to be listened to. *Wait a minute,* it said. *Howard has opened his soul to you, become vulnerable to you, listened to you—just as you wanted him to. He has told you he wants to become a better man. In turn, you have dug down into your own soul to understand your part in all of this. All of this has been in service of something larger than either of you: your marriage. That entity, into which you both entered blindly, has developed a life of its own—and that life is greater than you.*

These thoughts literally knocked the wind out of me. I had to sit down on the steps because I could no longer stand. As I sat there, I was not thinking logically or trying to figure anything out. I was flooded with the knowledge that I was in love with my husband and—perhaps more importantly—in love with our marriage. I wanted him back by my side.

Words cannot express the blinding certainty of it, but I will compare it to being engulfed by a tsunami and living to tell the tale. At that moment, I knew that I could and would bring Howard back into my heart.

While our marriage journey included many tenuous moments, our chemistry never wavered. It was present in its nascent form on our first date, developed in complexity and depth over the course of our marriage, and lasted until he died.

Once, in our early years, Howard and I were at a party that included couples young and old. I watched the older couples, some of whom had been married for many decades, dance together. *How sweet,* I thought, not yet understanding how one's perspective changes over a lifetime together and how a relationship grows because of it. Those older couples had depths of understanding that Howard and I had to achieve in our own time and our own way. The time that passed as we grew together, then apart, and finally together again was what made it possible for us to "fill our cracks with gold" rather than tossing away the cracked and battered object that our life had become.

Howard and I danced beside those older couples, experiencing our own particular chemistry and presuming it would never change. The older couples beside us were dancing a different dance—whether we appreciated that or not.

And, once Howard and I had recommitted to our marriage, our dance resumed with new depth and purpose, as if there had been no pause for pain or doubt, and continued throughout the rest of our journey together.

PART 3

THE NEXT TWENTY YEARS

"Building is a lot more fun than fixing."
—Bob Iger, CEO, The Walt Disney Company

I t was only as a result of our entire life experience, particularly the difficult decisions we made at age forty-seven, that Howard and I were able to have what outsiders saw as a great marriage. Most only remember those last twenty years, from our late forties to our late sixties, because our friends were all as busy as we were and absorbed in their own lives. On just one hand, I can count the number of people who knew the details of what happened between us.

I have written about the particulars of my life with Howard—especially the difficult ones—as a way of exemplifying the three concepts I believe underpin all long-term marriages:

- It has a life of its own.

- It is greater than the sum of its parts.
- It becomes a "third entity" separate from its two members.

To a large extent, it was our understanding of these three concepts that made our final decades great. Perhaps you can see why I think every challenge can be an opportunity and is therefore worthwhile.

By recognizing the aha moment when I was ready, willing, and able to recommit to Howard, I paved the way for us to maximize our lives as individuals and as a couple. I knew at that point that we could each be strong and follow our individual paths while creating new and greater opportunities together. Once we agreed to do that, we came together and began a new phase of our lives. I have decided to end this book by sharing that part of our journey: our "happily ever after."

CHAPTER 13

THE LIGHTNING BOLT HITS—NOW WHAT?

"Grow old along with me! The best is yet to be,
the last of life, for which the first was made."

—Robert Browning, English poet

O nce Howard and I agreed that we had to move forward in order to move together, we understood that we were about to enter a new phase of our lives. But how to begin? With baby steps. By sitting on the bench we had been sharing for the past three months, where we knew we would feel safe.

It was almost as if we were growing up again, but this time, with a lot of knowledge and experience under our belts. One thing we understood was that the only constant in life is change. We were both ready to take responsibility for our own actions—good, bad, and ugly. We acknowledged that our history incorporated many cracks and crevices, and that we would have to cement those together with a resin that included gold.

As we sat on that bench for what seemed like the thousandth time, I reminded Howard of a beloved quote by author Fawn Weaver: "Happiness in marriage is a moment by moment choice. A decision to love, forgive, grow, and grow old together." We vowed to honor those words by doing those very things.

Slowly, our bench conversation turned pragmatic, as in, "Now what do we do?" Howard brought up the idea of taking a short trip somewhere peaceful yet familiar.

"Without too much stress, please," he added. "Since we don't have to take any children with us, we can go somewhere and just share meals, be together, and take it easy."

Most people reading this might have trouble understanding what I said next, but Howard did not.

"Let's go back," I declared. "Let's begin again where we first began."

I wanted to make new memories, of course, but I also wanted to recall the fun and laughter of the time before life's challenges occurred and changed us. I hoped that maybe, like Dorothy in *The Wizard of Oz,* we could go back to Kansas—or in our case, New York. Maybe we could recreate that ride through Central Park on the night we got engaged—minus the itching and the drunken carriage driver. We could walk and walk, stopping at our favorite benches along the way.

When I finished laying out my vision, Howard just smiled and said, "You got it."

And so it began, our first step moving toward a better life. Within a month, he had bought plane tickets and reserved three nights in a hotel. The rest we would figure out in the moment.

Before long, we were back "home." Once we had settled into our hotel, we made a beeline for the Central Park carousel. Riding it round and round to the goofy calliope music had always made us smile, and this time was no different. Next came dinner at a delicatessen. I have always believed there are few problems that cannot be solved by sharing a genuine New York corned beef sandwich, and I think you would be hard-pressed to prove me wrong.

The next day, we were off to Radio City Music Hall to witness the perfect synchronicity of the famous Rockettes. Afterward, over hot chocolate, Howard reflected on the particular magic of the precision dancers. "Imagine how much work it takes to come together like that!" he marveled. Smiling, I could not help pointing out that their artistry could be viewed as a symbol of our own hard work with the same goal in mind.

Over a second cup of hot chocolate, I remembered an interview I had seen with Christine Lagarde, the former head of the International Monetary Fund, current head of the European Central Bank, and an integral member of the "table club" I referred to earlier in this book.

"What you said about the Rockettes reminds me of what Lagarde said about her own experience with synchronized swimming," I noted. "She explained that the sport had taught her how to be a member of a team and to work hard within a group to produce a spectacular result. She said that she went on to apply this same approach to leading teams of executives. I guess between the Rockettes and the leader of a world bank, we have some good role models!"

On the last day of our trip, we strolled through the city and made an unplanned stop at a small, tucked-away museum that had advertised a special exhibit of Tiffany stained glass. "Can you believe we've come across *this?*" said Howard, without any need to make reference to our own stained-glass *Welcome* sign. It was the universe at work!

That trip proved an effective first step in our new life together; it was exactly what we needed. Upon returning to Miami, we continued to enjoy our morning routine of coffee on the bench. In fact, we continued it for the rest of our time together. Each day, after we had talked and sipped our coffee to the dregs, we each went our own way to fulfill our individual responsibilities.

First New York, Now the World

Perhaps it is not surprising to you, since we clearly enjoyed our routines and traditions, that our long weekend in New York became an annual affair. "Sometimes, you know, it's necessary to go backward in order to go forward," Howard pointed out on one of them, quoting Martin Luther King Jr. and reminding me of our love of ballroom dancing.

We may have put New York on repeat, but each trip was unique. We made a point of stepping out of our comfort zone and exploring a new neighborhood each year, expanding our knowledge of an endlessly fascinating city and experiencing a bit of adventure.

After a few years, when our children were well on their way to being independent adults, Howard suggested we add an additional trip each year. "Think of all the places you want to go," he said, "and I'll do the planning."

I love bed-and-breakfasts, with their plentiful early morning meals and afternoon tea (sometimes wine), which provide a respite during the day's travel. Thus, we agreed that those would be part of the experience where possible. The conversations we had on our travels are some of my most cherished memories of my life with Howard.

We had friends in Sweden, Portugal, and Australia, so we started there and took advantage of their wonderful guidance and hospitality. Then came Paris, which was high on my wish list but where we knew no one.

You either "get" Paris or you do not. On our first trip there, Howard did not. "Maybe we should give it a second shot," I said after we got back. I had loved it so much, I just hoped he would learn to love it as well. And guess what? He did. And I think it made him trust my instincts more as we continued our travel planning. We ended up going back to Paris a number of times, and, as we did in New York, continually broadened our horizons—from the divine artwork at the marvelous Musée d'Orsay to the mystical Père-Lachaise Cemetery, where we contemplated the tombs of Frédéric Chopin, Honoré de Balzac, Oscar Wilde, and Jim Morrison. It was there that we rediscovered forest bathing while sitting on a shady bench, quietly appreciating our surroundings.

Of course, our life together was not all vacations. At home, we learned to live consciously in both our personal and professional spheres, and how to balance the two without letting stress overtake joy. It did not hurt that our children were launched or that, as we aged, it was easier to keep our work lives in perspective.

We are like bookends, which do not always perfectly align. Just like adjusting a set of bookends to support a row of books, it may take some trial and error for two individuals to redistribute their weight and make the changes necessary to find the right balance in their relationship. Each of us is unique, but when we find equilibrium, we can both contribute equally toward our shared goals.

Our marriage continued to evolve as we built upon our strengths, and gradually, the pain of the past receded and became something for which we were honestly grateful. If we had not experienced that pain, we would never have appreciated the pleasure of waking up each day to our new life together.

CHAPTER 14

THE THREE-RING CIRCUS

"Life is a great big beautiful three-ring circus. There are those on the floor making their lives among the heads of lions and hoops of fire, and those in the stands, complacent and wowed, their mouths stuffed with popcorn."

—Christopher Hawke, *Unnatural Truth*

A three-ring circus can be spectacular, tumultuous, and a little confusing. Constantly shifting one's gaze from ring to ring in order to capture every raucous moment can be exhausting; there is just too much going on! Perhaps it is fun for an afternoon, but most of us need more structure in our day-to-day lives—more organization and more moments of peace.

After experiencing the "three-ring circus" of our own lives, Howard and I came to believe there was a way to see it not simply as chaos but as something more positive. If you really study a circus, you will find that, in spite of all the moving pieces, there is an underlying order that comes from practice and cooperation.

Our three rings consisted of our marriage, our children, and our work. Though disparate, those rings did intersect, and

Howard and I stood like co-ringmasters at the point of intersection. It was our job to manage all the "acts," provide direction and reassurance, and keep the show moving forward harmoniously.

During the last phase of our life together, we learned to do that well by listening, communicating, and working in tandem. We could now solve problems as they arose, even when confronted by multiple challenges simultaneously.

The result was a measure of calm we had never enjoyed at earlier times in our marriage. There was room for reflection, planning, and sharing. Stresses that might have caused those fateful cracks of our earlier years could be discussed and dispelled rather than left to widen and imperil the whole.

I am not saying that our process was always easy; the life we had committed to involved courage and determination on both our parts. Was it worth it? I think you know my answer to that.

Ring One: Our Marriage

Once Howard and I had committed to putting each other's happiness ahead of our own, we experienced the kind of joy I believe can only be found in a long-term committed relationship. Howard no longer had to be the one and only main character in our life together. He had repaired his relationships—with me and everyone else—and was now enjoying being a member of each circle he belonged to rather than having to be at its center. He listened more carefully and loved being loved. While we still felt mutual infatuation, we also grew to appreciate the more conscious and thoughtful aspects of being together. We genuinely enjoyed listening to each other's perspectives on all kinds of things, from the personal to the political to the aesthetic. We never ceased to appreciate the importance of words and reflected on Solomon's dramatic pronouncement, as recorded in the book of Proverbs, that "the tongue has the power of life and death." Quite simply, by encouraging each other, we inspired courage *in* each other.

Just as they had done in our earliest years, romantic gestures came easily. Our hands touched more freely, our kisses came more frequently, and our glances communicated love and admiration. We easily succumbed to the following lyrics by Cynthia Weil: "Just a little lovin' early in the mornin' beats a cup of coffee for starting out the day."

Neither of us felt the need to continually rehash the past, though our awareness of our history and what we had almost lost informed everything we did and said. The primary focus was on *us* now, not our children or our colleagues. We prioritized ourselves as a unit, even going so far as to reinstitute the date nights we had enjoyed as young marrieds.

Ring Two: Our Children

Beginning with those initial difficult conversations with each of his children, Howard began to develop the respect for them that comes from truly listening. In turn, they regained their trust in him even as they developed adult lives and relationships of their own. When his role as a mentor was needed, he offered guidance. When it was he who needed support, he learned how to ask for it and accept it. The result was that we grew closer to our children than we had been since they had become adults. And it was not just Howard's behavior that changed; I, too, learned how to let go of them while holding on tight. We no longer felt like guests in their homes, nor did they feel like guests in ours.

Over the years, our children have occasionally referred to us as role models for marriage. While this may sound a bit arrogant, we are able to accept this compliment because each of them has been married for over twenty years. Of course, each of their journeys will continue to have its own unique challenges and triumphs.

Then came the grandchildren and with them, an even broader perspective. When Howard and I first became parents, he was a marvelous father, devoting endless time and attention to his children as if from some deep instinct. Seeing him with his grandchildren brought all of that back to me, and I marveled at his innate parenting (now grandparenting) skills all over again.

Now he could truly immerse himself in all aspects of family life, and this melted my heart. It seemed that this was the gold that would finally seal our cracks permanently. Sometimes, we would take our grandchildren for an early morning breakfast at the local International House of Pancakes. Afterward, Howard would drop me back at the house so I could spend time with Mara while he and the grandchildren went to the park. Later, he would drop off the little ones with us so he could spend some "guy time" with Tracey. I am happy to report that my son-in-law always had time for my husband.

On one occasion, Howard made the unilateral decision to take the little ones on an airboat ride in the Everglades instead of their usual trip to the park. They began shouting that they did not want to go. Tracey was not far from earshot, but by the time he could see what was happening, Howard had scooped them up with "no mosquito repellent, no long sleeves, and most importantly, no permission!" Off they went, tears and all.

Tracey immediately called Mara, frantically shouting, "Your father has kidnapped the children!"

There was nothing Mara and I could do but hope for the best.

A few hours later, they returned. Tracey just stood there speechless, as the children were now smiling, laughing, and full of stories to share of this grand adventure with Grandpa, who was now their hero! Mara and Tracey had no choice but to develop a great deal of patience for these New York-style grandparents.

Ring Three: Our Work

Howard's professional relationships continued to develop over the next twenty years because he now appreciated that each member of his team was essential. Howard grew to understand journalist Sebastian Junger's idea that "humans don't mind hardship; in fact, they thrive on it. What they mind is not feeling necessary. Modern society has perfected the art of making people not feel necessary." Each of his colleagues had his or her own strengths and skills that benefited the patients and, ultimately, the practice.

Every morning, before the office opened for business, Howard and the staff gathered and spent time together. They did so again at lunchtime. As Howard's understanding of people's work needs deepened, he learned to provide encouragement and positive reinforcement, and he soon began to take pleasure in doing so. It is no surprise that the practice became more successful each year. The best part is that Howard began to share these increasing profits with his employees. The holidays became a time of joy and festivity when gifts were exchanged and bonuses were offered, along with Howard's genuine gratitude.

As part of the holiday celebrations, Howard spent real time and effort arranging a surprise day of fun for the staff. He would hire a limousine and send them off on a shopping spree or to a spa—whichever activity he felt they would genuinely enjoy.

Another occasion for generosity came each June, just before the start of the next fiscal year. At that time, Howard would thoughtfully share additional bonuses reflective of the year's profits, and they were often enough to make a real difference in the lives of his employees. I recall one of his assistants buying a coveted refrigerator and another going on a dream vacation with her husband. As important as the extra money was to them, even more valuable was the tangible proof of their value to Howard and the business. It was certainly meaningful to me as I watched from the sidelines.

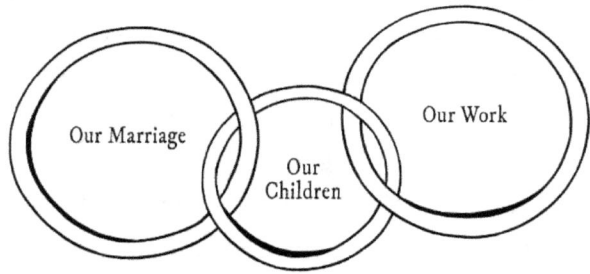

An Alchemical Process Evolves

The three Japanese concepts I described in detail—kintsugi (making something useful again by honoring its history), wabi-sabi (appreciating and accepting the imperfection in life), and ikigai (having a sense of purpose and reason for living)— continued to guide us as we moved forward. In fact, they became central to our life together.

In the first ring, our marriage, we came to understand the concept of kintsugi. Over the next twenty years, whenever we referred back to the effort we had put into helping each other, even through our failures, we would reference a quote by author Gary Chapman: "The best thing we can do with failures of the past is to let them be history. We can choose to live today free from the failures of yesterday." It was our time to revisit the dance, to smile, to be close, and to value the present as our golden moment.

In the second ring, our children, we focused on wabi-sabi, sharing with our children the lessons we had learned about life and its challenges. Acceptance of our imperfections had made us stronger, and we knew that with our guidance, it could make them stronger as well.

In the third ring, our work, we focused on ikigai and the inherent sense of purpose that arises from passion for one's profession. We understood how fortunate we were to get up each morning to work at something we loved, and we were both eager to put forth our best efforts to do our jobs well and help others.

With our three rings in mind, and the three philosophical concepts we believed in, we stood proudly at the intersection of our busy lives, knowing that together we could face all challenges and help those we cared about to do the same.

CHAPTER 15

EMPTY NESTERS

"Never let a good crisis go to waste."

—Sir Winston Churchill, British military leader and statesman

W e were not about to let one moment of our time to-gether get lost. As empty nesters, we were now the main characters of our story, and we wanted to base the final chapters of it on two things: logic and magic. These would form the foundation on which we would rebuild our love affair.

Fortunately, we were both passionate about our careers as well as each other and had saved enough money to live without fear. We did not have to fret too much about whether or when to retire, or whether we would have enough money to live as we wished. We could focus on building our connection and mutual trust, and living the best and most selfless lives possible. We both continued to grow as professionals without the need to move up the ladder; instead, we focused on getting better at what we did. Believe it or not, that in itself was exciting for us. At home, we continued to express ourselves and our love through music, dance, and precious family time.

When we looked back from that point, it seemed to us that we had spent years standing in a slow-moving line, waiting our turn at the ice cream counter. Now we were at the front of the line, making our selections and enjoying every bite. Was the long wait worth it? You bet it was! We had no idea (I do not think anyone ever does) how long this new period would last—that it would be limited to just twenty years. I am happy to say that we danced through most of them.

How we looked at things as a couple was essential. As the years went by, the challenges that presented themselves did not seem as monumental. We chose to approach them as learning experiences. We had disagreements sometimes, but those, too, became learning experiences. As Leonard Cohen, poet and songwriter, put it: "There is a crack in everything. That's how the light gets in." We both felt humbled by the possibility of dwelling always in the positive rather than letting negativity chip away at our connection. The house was blissfully quiet and peaceful in a way we had not known we craved.

At the beginning of this period of rebirth, we sometimes felt like teenagers sneaking out late at night. We would take a drive for a cup of Miami's best *café con leche* or an ice cream. Some evenings, we would place the dinner I had prepared in the refrigerator and head out for sloppy joes consumed on our favorite bench. The world was open to us, and we embraced our spontaneity.

As it always had been, travel was an integral part of our marriage. We were very good at managing our frequent-flier miles, but beyond that, we kept our travel plans loose and easy. Once, on a road trip in Northern California, we stopped at a highly recommended restaurant for an early lunch. Surprisingly, we were their only customers at that time. Our table faced the ocean, the view was spectacular, and the fresh food exceeded our expectations. As we exited the restaurant, we noticed a lounge area where music was playing—Louis Armstrong's "What a Wonderful World." We just smiled and started dancing. When the music ended and we looked up, standing in a line watching us were about seven employees. Some were servers, some were kitchen staff, and all were clapping. We might have been a bit embarrassed, but there it was—another moment along our travels. They were young; we were not. Who enjoyed the moment more? We will never know.

We had never been tour bus types and had become adept at exploring new places on our own (granted, with a little help from Rick Steves's travel guides and guided walking tours of local sites). In small towns, we enjoyed watching street musicians (occasionally dancing along), admiring works by local artists, people-watching, and sampling local treats. On one occasion, we spent a few days in the quiet village of Varenna, Italy. We stayed in an old monastery near the area where most visitors ferried in and out. Each day, after our daily jaunts, we stopped by

Varenna's version of 7-Eleven and sat outside. Locals—including the mayor, various workmen, and housekeepers—gathered there to enjoy inexpensive, not-so-delicious wine, chips, and conversation. Howard and I enjoyed watching their interactions and listening to their lively banter, even though we did not understand their language.

After several afternoons, no one paid much attention to us as they listened carefully to one another, laughing and sharing. One day, a housekeeper carrying a large box got off the bus and joined the group. Everyone gathered around her, anxious to view its contents. She opened the box and extracted a brand-new carpet sweeper. Everyone swooned. What was so interesting to us was how happy everyone was for her. They actually clapped! It was obvious this community of friends had mastered sharing the joy, the moment. We learned a great deal that afternoon as we watched the best part of people caring for one another unfold before us. After two decades of joyful, eye-opening trips, I am grateful for the detailed journals I kept, which allow me to revisit and relive all those fond memories.

Rediscovering the Pool

Having a private pool is a great pleasure—especially when you have a growing extended family. Howard and I relished watching our children and grandchildren splash around and have fun together, and I still do. I always have an ample supply of fresh towels, sunscreen, and cold drinks, and no matter how old the kids get, I still keep an eye on them every second they are in the water.

One day during this new period of our lives, Howard asked me to come outside and help him bring some things in from the trunk of the car. When I took a look, I saw two large, dark-blue pool rafts, the fancy kind with cupholders on the sides. "These are just for us," he declared.

There are basically only two seasons in Miami, hot and hotter, and those "grown-up rafts" got a lot of use when nobody was visiting. We would float around lazily, lightly splashing each other, listening to music, and laughing as the rafts gently collided. When we had enough, I would prepare tuna sandwiches, fresh fruit, and water bottles, and we would sit on the pool steps with our bottoms in the water, enjoying our picnic.

We never got tired of that activity and came to think of our life—for at least the five months of oppressive heat and humidity—as float, relax, repeat!

Empty Nesters Being Silly

Howard and I decided it might be nice to create a fun experience that included our fellow empty nesters. It was the late '90s, and I hit upon the idea of a TV show-themed party. "Go for it!" Howard exclaimed. "Just tell me what you need me to do."

I enlisted the help of some friends who shared our stage of life, saying, "Let's work together to create something fun without worrying about whether we're 'too old' for this kind of nonsense."

They looked at me, puzzled but intrigued.

"You know that show *Dynasty?*" I asked, referring to a popular nighttime soap opera that had recently ended on a cliffhanger, leaving viewers as angry as hornets. Ultimately, the network bowed under the pressure and announced that there would be a one-night finale. It was coming up in two months.

My friends, most of whom considered the show a guilty pleasure, nodded.

I went on to suggest that we throw a watch party for that grand finale. I would host and arrange for catered food, and everyone else could take on a task. When one friend contacted CBS and shared our plan, the station manager informed her that there were similar parties being planned throughout the country (who would have thought?) and that they would provide us with photos and life-size cardboard cutouts of the cast.

The swag soon arrived, and we placed the cast photos on top of framed pictures of my own family members so it would look as though my home was their home. We positioned the cardboard figures by the front door and had a photographer (one of my friends) with a Polaroid camera ready to take shots of our guests alongside them. The photos printed instantly, and everyone had a souvenir to take home.

Another friend recorded the show's theme song and was responsible for playing it as each guest entered the house. Another person, who happened to sell floor coverings for a living, donated a long red carpet that we laid from the driveway to the front door. Another, who was prominent in local politics, offered the use of a limousine to be parked outside for effect. My husband had two patients who were uniformed police officers, and they stationed themselves on either side of our door as "security."

The night was clear and crisp, the food was delicious, and everyone dressed up. Forty grown-ups, mostly empty nesters like us, had a ball playing make-believe and walked away with great memories. To this day, anyone who attended the Sacks *Dynasty* party still remembers the evening with delight.

Food—The Great Connector

For Howard and me, sharing a meal was always a good opportunity for an extended conversation that often yielded new ideas. Obviously, we ate to stay healthy, feed our family, and occasionally socialize with others. But now, everything was a conscious choice, and mealtime was no different. We put effort into making it surprising and fun.

When Howard walked in the door with a fragrant bag of bagels and lox—my favorite meal—it was his way of putting my happiness first. The same was true when he would plan a trip to a special deli for another one of my favorites, derma. (Most delicatessens no longer serve this dish, and if you google it, you might gag—but I assure you, it is delicious and has the added benefit for me of conjuring up wonderful memories of my mother and dear Aunt Pearlie.)

These acts of thoughtfulness were not a one-way street between us. I was aware, for example, that Howard loved food served from trucks on the street, especially Greek souvlaki drenched in thick, white tzatziki sauce. I made sure to work that into our routine when I could, and I never failed to be amused by the inevitable dribbles of sauce on Howard's shirt afterward.

As time went on, we began to include friends on our excursions to out-of-the-way restaurants. One morning on my way to work, I stopped for gas and a coffee and discovered a most unusual restaurant at the rear of the large gas station. All I could make out in the dim light within was a large number of wine bottles and a long wooden table that appeared to seat at least twenty. (You will recall that big wooden tables hold special significance for me.)

I asked the manager about the place, and in response, he turned the lights up for me. I was amazed to find myself standing inside a cozy restaurant that could have been in a European city, with hundreds of wines from around world and a large menu on a chalkboard featuring international dishes from Spain, Portugal, Italy, and France.

"Thank you!" I exclaimed. "I'll be back!"

I called Howard from the car to share what I had discovered, and that weekend, off we went with some adventurous friends. As I had hoped, the meal and the experience were incredible.

This hidden gem was eventually discovered by the media and ended up winning an award for the best wine bar in Miami. We continued to enjoy meals there even after it was "discovered," without ever having to stand in the long lines that formed, as the manager remembered us and always ushered us right in. I will never know if it was fate taking care of us or that wooden table.

Howard and I loved to entertain at home as well. When our friends celebrated anniversaries or birthdays, we would prepare special dinners served on our best dishes atop fancy tablecloths. We would listen to good music and end the meals with rich desserts, fruits, and cheeses. It was our way of honoring our friends and recognizing that just because we were empty nesters did not mean our house ever had to be empty.

The Moments

Most of the fun and frivolous things we treated ourselves to during those last two decades together would not have been possible at earlier times in our lives, either due to financial constraints or lack of time. In addition to a wide range of dining adventures, we enjoyed some unparalleled arts performances, including theater, ballet, opera, and symphony. In the beginning, we sat in the nose-bleed section, but as the years went by, we moved closer to the stage.

I had always been a fan of the actor Paul Newman, and when Howard saw that he would be coming to Broadway in a nine-week limited production of *Our Town*, he immediately bought us tickets—and not just any tickets. There I sat, a few months later, in the front row, feeling as if Paul were speaking directly to me. Howard was by my side, of course, but there was no question this treat was for me.

I did not think he could ever top that—but he managed. After a twenty-seven-year absence from the stage, Barbra Streisand announced she would be doing a small tour—just five cities. Howard arranged for us to fly to Washington, DC, for the occasion, and I could not have been more thrilled. Barbra did not disappoint, and neither did the crowd. Most of Congress was present, as were President Clinton and the First Lady. It was a once-in-a-lifetime event—until it was not. A few years later, Barbra performed her final concert at Madison Square Garden. Once again, we were there, and once again, I was certain the performance was directed at me!

Upon our leaving the concert, an electrifying moment occurred. On the Times Square Megatron, they replayed Streisand's last songs, performed just moments prior. Something happened I had never seen before and have not since. All traffic heading down Broadway outside Madison Square Garden came to a dead halt. People got out of their cars, sat on the hoods, and sang along. When it was over, they got back into their cars and continued driving. Where else could this have happened, and for whom else?

CHAPTER 16

DANCING THAT LAST DANCE

*"And those who were seen dancing were thought to
be insane by those who could not hear the music."*

—Friedrich Nietzsche, German philosopher

Along with some friends, we enjoyed our tenth trip to
Sweden. Each of those annual trips was then capped by
a visit to a different country in Northern Europe.

While planning that trip to Scandinavia, Howard said to
me, "This time, pick a special place you would like to see again."
Neither of us realized that would be our last trip anywhere. So,
when he asked me to pick one of the places I most enjoyed visiting,
he was actually being almost prophetic, without even realizing it—
one of life's ironies. Without hesitation I responded, "The Vigeland
Sculpture Park in Oslo, Norway."

This beautiful place contains over two hundred granite,
bronze, and wrought-iron sculptures representing human life.
I have thought about it many times since we had first visited. At
the time, I thought Howard was simply being thoughtful. In retrospect, I cannot help viewing his decision as prophetic.

The trip was all we had hoped it would be, and the sculpture park was as magical as I had remembered. We came home with new memories to layer upon the old and were eager to begin planning our next adventure.

It all ended in a moment. Shortly after our return to Miami, we went to the doctor for our annual checkups. The results changed our lives forever. We received the news that no one ever wants to hear, and we entered a new phase of our lives in an instant.

We consulted several specialists and, ultimately, sought advice from the country's leading researcher on Howard's disease. The doctor happened to practice in California, so we grabbed the first appointment we could get and took an overnight flight.

After introductions, the doctor began the visit by saying, "Dr. Sacks, I have reviewed all your medical records and the results of your lab work. I know you are as aware of your prognosis as I am. My goal is to teach you to 'dance backward.'"

Had I heard him correctly? After our exhausting overnight flight and mad dash through an unfamiliar city, all this specialist had to offer us was some nonsense about dancing backward?!

"As you know," he continued, looking from Howard to me and back again, "the disease will keep coming at you, and ultimately, it will win. But I think I can help you move backward as it moves forward. There are ways we can prolong your life if you're willing to dance with this horrid disease. Do you know how to dance?"

Suddenly, a frisson of electricity overcame me. I immediately knew we were in the *right* place. Howard and I had begun our life together by dancing, and we had danced through the ups and downs of our middle and later years. Dancing was what we did, and we were not going to stop now. Clearly, the universe had carried us to where we needed to be.

This specialist helped us dance right up to the end—an end that arrived later than anyone had predicted. I suppose we were the embodiment of artist Vivian Green's notion that "life isn't about waiting for the storm to pass. It's about learning to dance in the rain."

In this final segment of our lives, all that Howard had learned during the hardest period of our life together came into play. Over the last nine months of his life, he chose to take care of me by preparing me for my life ahead. Though already bedridden, he calmly explained that there were things he wanted to teach me—things I would need to know because he would not be around to take care of them. And that is exactly what he did!

I have already written a whole book about Howard's last days and my subsequent life as a widow, so I will summarize what happened only briefly here. Suffice it to say that my ability to move forward without him was eased greatly by his careful tutelage, and I consider this his last great gift to me.

Step by step, with patience and all of his waning strength, Howard schooled me in investment matters and the stock market. I cannot say I was the best pupil in this area, but I did learn how to save up each year for the house insurance and taxes, how to transfer his accrued airline miles so that I could use them, how to put the car in my name, and many other details of our personal business.

He also shared his wishes regarding his gravesite. He wanted me to purchase a bench and a mature tree. I was to place the bench near his grave and have the tree planted so that it would shade the bench from the sun for me or anyone else who sat there, just as in the Greek proverb, "A society grows great when old men plant trees in whose shade they shall never sit." While honoring these requests, I realized he was still taking care of *me*.

When I expressed my apprehension about staying in our large house alone, he told me I could do it—and *should* do it—if that was what I wanted. "People will advise you to sell the house," he said, "but don't listen to them. Do what feels right for you."

He was correct about all of the well-meaning people who advised me to move, and he was right to tell me to follow my heart. I figured out how to stay in our beautiful home and—step by step—how to maintain it, and I have never regretted that decision for a moment.

Epilogue

The Hope Chest

As an avid reader who fell under the spell of old English and French romance novels as a girl, I was fascinated by the notion of a hope chest. For those of you who have never heard of such a thing (they are a bit out of style nowadays), a hope chest is an actual wooden chest given to a girl of marriageable age, in which she can store her trousseau—all of the bedding, clothing, and other items she will need as a married lady. For many young women of my generation, having a hope chest meant having hope!

During the first three years Howard and I dated, we collected all kinds of mementos and souvenirs, from ticket stubs and playbills to restaurant menus and cocktail napkins. After four years, we got engaged, and I told him I wanted a hope chest in which to store our treasures.

Instead of purchasing something ready-made, we found a wood craftsman in New York's East Village, which was in those days a bohemian enclave full of artists and artisans (and, from the smell of its streets, quite a few pot smokers). We ended up ordering a medium-sized chest made of pine, the least expensive option the man offered. In two months, it was ready, and I eagerly brought it home to Queens.

The reason I bring this up is that I want to end by telling you about the very first thing I put in my hope chest. While in college, Howard and I liked to take leisurely car rides to poke around in small towns. (This is something we would continue to do throughout our life together.) On one of these jaunts, we stopped for a light lunch in a Long Island hamlet and strolled along its main street afterward. In the window of a little boutique, I noticed a lovely pale-green cotton skirt. The price tag was all too visible and read either $12 or $18. Whichever it was, it was considerably more than my $7 weekly allowance. We walked on.

The next week, when Howard picked me up for a date, he was carrying a flat white box tied with a shiny white ribbon. I am sure you know what was in it.

Later that night, I placed the first items in my hope chest—not the pretty green skirt, which went into my closet and was worn on numerous occasions over many years, but the flat white box and the shiny white ribbon.

To this day, those items sit at the very bottom of the chest, covered by layer upon layer of keepsakes that represent a lifetime of adventure, fun, and love. At the top lies a death certificate representing the end of that life together. Between the flat white box and the death certificate . . . that is our marriage. If you were to look at it, you would see a pile of papers and trinkets. What I see is pure gold.

> "Your life at this exact moment is a direct result of choices you made once upon a time."
> —Sarah Ban Breathnach, author

Afterword

Golden Nuggets Collected Along Our Yellow Brick Road

I do not come to you as a marriage expert or pundit who provides authoritative opinions or advice. However, I do come to you as one who has learned. I share this learning through my story, our story. This book was written after much reflection on a relationship of half a century, beginning with the naïveté of youth and ending with the wisdom attained through age. There is a beginning, a middle, and an end.

In writing this book, I discovered that the number three repeatedly appeared as we navigated our life together. This powerful number is often associated with communication skills, the ability to build myriad relationships, and finding creative solutions that others tend to overlook. I did not plan this recurring theme; it evolved just as we did.

- I developed three ways to look at marriage: alchemy, the Greeks' six stages of love, and fairy tales.

- I applied three concepts to our marriage: Marriage has a life of its own. The whole is greater than the sum of its parts. And marriage is a third entity.
- I divided our lives and our story into three parts: the early years, the middle years, and the later years.
- We operated in our own three-ring circus: The first ring was composed of our marriage. The second ring was composed of our children. And the third ring was composed of our work.
- We learned and embedded three Japanese philosophies that added understanding and depth to our lives: kintsugi, wabi-sabi, and ikigai.
- Howard crafted three objects during the early years that still remain with me: an oak table (there were three members in the "table club"), a stained- glass *Welcome* sign, and an oak rolltop desk.

As I journeyed through my fifty years with Howard, this book evolved into a collection of stories. I was gobsmacked, so very astounded by the fact that learning to love your spouse is a process, a lifetime of choices that are different from those in any other relationship. I grew to understand that the word love, which applies to so many friendships and relationships, is notably distinct when it comes to marriage.

There are many aspects of relationships that are comforting. However, Howard and I discovered that in marriage there are fears, challenges, and situations that can create difficult paths. To complicate things even further, there is no one path, no one journey. By traveling our unique journey together, we grew to understand that some unexpected situations were just pebbles along our road, while others were frightening boulders, often hard to navigate around. Some appeared when our nucleus was just two. A number of them originated from external sources; some came from our family, and others were the result of social change. For all of them, we had to make choices and decisions in order to overcome challenging realities. I guess that is to be expected in a relationship of over half a century, which comes with no road map or navigation system.

Our stories span from simple to complex, from happy to sad, from our beginning to our end. Hopefully, you can find a story in your own relationship that helps you move together. On occasion, one has to decide which is more important: being right or being together. Discovering the balance between magic and logic may help you get there.

Our story is an illustration of how this might look. Each of our stages of love contributed to the total picture, which formed a new perspective for the two of us. This took us a long time, but such a journey made our marriage stronger and clearer as it became its own entity. It may take you a lifetime to reach that point and remain there as you continue to dance through your life together. You may ask, what is it when you get there? It is everything!

Once again, I thank you for sharing my journey, and I wish you well along yours.

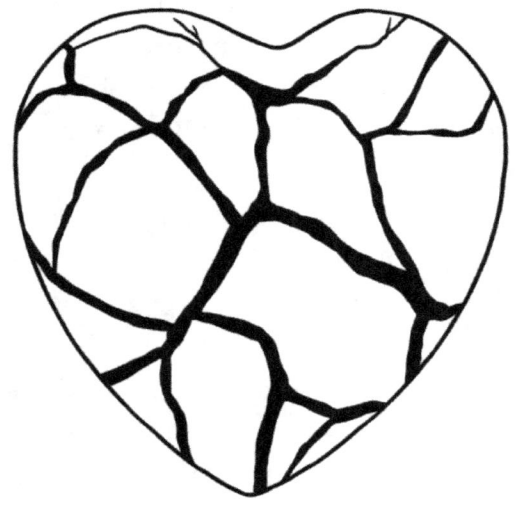

Acknowledgments

While it is the magic of the muse that inspires you and ignites your passion, it is the logic and reality provided by those in your life who move you forward, every day, in every way.

It is my privilege to acknowledge the strong, independent women who patiently contributed to my journey in writing this book. First, my gratitude is to my most competent and concerned daughter, Mara, who provided support every day for two and a half years during the creation of this work; thus, I was able to follow my dream.

There are others who walked this path with me as well. Each patiently listened, understood (even if they really did not), and helped me process daily challenges. Some took long walks with me, some shared a café or that afternoon glass of wine; some tried to chew their food as I rambled on at dinners, some spent hours on the phone from long distances . . . each and every one providing a positive space in order for me to fill that space with my thoughts and words.

Just as I have shared my concept in this book that marriage is a balance between magic and logic, I believe it is also a combination of magic (provided by my muse) and logic (provided by these women).

It is with the greatest appreciation that I thank you all.

Arlene Sacks

Discussion Questions

If you are reading this book as part of a book club or reading group, below are some discussion questions to help the conversation. If not, feel free to skip this portion.

1. How did the characters change or grow throughout the story?

2. What would you do if you were in this place? As Arlene? As Howard?

3. In today's society, would this marriage have had the same outcome? Why or why not?

4. Do you agree or disagree with the three concepts: marriage has a life of its own, the whole is greater than the

sum of its parts, and the marriage is a third entity? Why or why not?

5. Do you agree or disagree with the idea that marriage is a balance between logic and magic? Why or why not?

6. What is your opinion on the Greeks' six stages of love? Do you believe you have to go through them all? Do you need to go through them in order?

7. How might the Greeks' six stages of love apply to your relationship?

8. How do you feel about the idea that love is a developmental process as well as a choice?

9. What do you think the author's main purpose for writing this book was? How does it impact your own life or reflection about your relationship?

10. Do you have your own "park bench"? If so, how did it come about, and what does it signify?

11. Which scene in this book has stuck with you the most?

12. The author divided her marriage into the early, middle, and later years in order to demonstrate how the cracks developed slowly. Do you think the initial cracks were purposely ignored? Why or why not?

13. Of the three Japanese philosophies, which resonated most with you: kintsugi, wabi-sabi, or ikigai? How might this impact your view of marriage? Were you aware of these three concepts prior to reading this book?

14. Are there any specific points you feel could have been further explored by the author?

15. What did you think of the author's voice and style? Did the quality of the writing match that of the stories she told?

16. Did you find the content in this book helpful for your current relationship, and if so, why? If not in a relationship at the moment, what tools has this book given you for future relationships?

17. Do you have any favorite quotes from the book?

18. Would you recommend this book to a friend? How would you summarize the story if you were to recommend it?

19. If you were given the chance to ask the author one question, what would it be?

About the Author

Born in New York City, as a child, Arlene enjoyed the carousel and greenery of Central Park, playgrounds, street fairs, and the city's free performances. As an adult, she developed a love for theater, museums, and the opportunity to sample the city's myriad ethnic foods. Currently, Miami is her home. She enjoys the diversity and excitement of the city. Arlene is involved in the writing community and is grateful for the opportunity to be part of a city that is continuously developing and making its mark worldwide.

Dr. Sacks studied education and psychology during her undergraduate and master's degree studies. In her doctoral studies, she focused on education and behavioral psychology as a student of B.F. Skinner's daughter. She has served as Director of Graduate Programs at St. Thomas University and Barry University, both in Miami, Florida. Additionally, she has been the Dean of Doctoral Programs and served as Associate Vice President of Academic Affairs at Union Institute & University, based in Cincinnati, Ohio.

Arlene has greatly enjoyed being a wife, mother, and grandmother and has been called a great storyteller. This is evidenced in her book *Moving Forward: The Widow's Journey*, in which she befriended and interviewed thirteen widows from diverse cultures who shared their stories about moving forward after loss.

Moving Forward: The Widow's Journey was named a finalist in the Foreword INDIES, the National Indie Excellence Awards, and was shortlisted in the 2022 Selfies Book Awards. If you would like to purchase a copy of her first book, please do so here.

www.ingramcontent.com/pod-product-compliance
Lightning Source LLC
Chambersburg PA
CBHW071358120626
46546CB00002B/742